Railway World **SPEC**

C000069439

DIDCOT

JUNCTION & RAILWAY CENTRE

LONDON

IAN ALLAN LTD

Laurence Waters

PRODUCED IN ASSOCIATION WITH THE GREAT WESTERN SOCIETY LTD

Contents

Acknowledgements
I would like to thank the following for their help in preparing this book: H. Cullen, Joe Turner, Tony Doyle, Brian Matthews, Brian Higgins, Dr Malcolm Graham, David Castle, Paul Cobb, David Koslow, Jeanette and Mick Howse, Mick Dean, David Martin, Peter Rance, Fred Gray, Bill Peto, Charles Whetmath, Frank Dumbleton, Peter Chatman and also the many other members of the workforce at Didcot who are too numerous to mention individually.

Front cover:
Two 'Halls' and a 'Manor' grace the front of Didcot shed; they are No 6998 *Burton Agnes Hall*, No 5900 *Hinderton Hall* and 7808 *Cookham Manor*. *Frank Dumbleton*

Right:
Society member Brian Thompson slowly eases No 3822 forward to the shed water column as the engine is prepared for another days work at Didcot. *Author*

First published 1989

ISBN 0 7110 1831 6

Published by Ian Allan Ltd, Shepperton, Surrey; and printed by Ian Allan Printing Ltd at their works at Coombelands in Runnymede, England

The Growth of the Railway at Didcot

Lying on a ridge between the Thames Valley to the north and the Hagbourne Hills to the south is the town of Didcot. Today it is impossible to miss Didcot with the six 350ft-high cooling towers of the CEGB power station completely dominating the surrounding area. The town currently has a population of some 14,000 inhabitants, which in the next few years is planned to expand to around 18,000. This is a far cry from the days before the arrival of the railway when Didcot, with a population of just 181, was the smallest village in the area. The name Didcot derives from 'Dud(d)a's cottage/cote'. In 1206 the name Dudecota was being used, and the change of 'u' to 'i' seems to date from about 1650. The present spelling appears to have first been used from about 1657. There have been, interestingly, no less than 22 derivatives of the name used over the years, with the current usage finally being settled on early in this century.

During the 16th century the village had almost ceased to exist when attempts were made to enclose the common land and convert all the arable land into pasture. The tenants at the time complained bitterly that it seemed to be the intention of the lords to pull down the whole village and to convert it into pasture. Luckily this did not happen and the small village survived. Even in 1801 the village comprised just five farms and a cluster of cottages around the church.

Didcot could not really be described as a railway town in the same sense as Swindon or Crewe, yet it owes its growth over the last 140 years or so almost entirely to the arrival of the Great Western Railway.

In 1824, almost a year before the opening of the Stockton & Darlington railway, a proposal was put forward by the London & Bristol Railroad Co for a line linking the two cities. The route proposed by this company was via Reading, Wallingford, Wantage and Mangotsfield. Had this line been built it would have passed some distance away from Didcot, but financial support was not forthcoming and the project was abandoned. The idea of a London to Bristol railway was revived once again in 1833, only this time by the Great Western Railway (GWR) Co, which of course was to appoint Isambard Kingdom

Brunel as its engineer. A new route was soon proposed that would take the line close to Didcot; the 1833 prospectus contained three possible branches, to Gloucester, Bradford-on-Avon and Oxford. Didcot appears to be mentioned for the first time in this document as the possible junction for the Oxford branch. A clue to the change of route from the 1824 proposal can be gleaned from the 1833 prospectus which stated 'The proposed line will pass through or near Slough, Maidenhead, Reading and Wantage. This line has been preferred on account of the superiority of its levels and the ultimate economy of working steam power on it, as well as offering the greatest facilities for a junction with Oxford'. This first proposal was however rejected by the House of Lords. A second proposal (which did not contain the branch to Oxford) was submitted by the company in 1835 and this time it proved to be successful and received Royal Assent on 31 August of the same year. On 29 October 1835 the company also took the decision to use a gauge of 7ft 0¼in for its new line.

Construction began in 1836, and with steady progress the line had reached Didcot by 1 June 1840, finally opened throughout to Bristol on 30 June 1841. Brunel apparently was so sure of the success of his new line that it is said he was prepared to wager the enormous sum of

Above:
This Measham drawing shows how Didcot Junction must have looked in 1852. Note the five platforms serving just four tracks, and the unusual design of the overall roof. *Author's collection*

£1,000 that, when completed, passengers would be transported from Bristol to London in just two hours. Because of the easy terrain, the cost of building the line from Didcot to Uffington was just £6,000/mile. This apparently was quite a low figure compared to the cost of some other lines. No station was provided at Didcot at this time, the nearest being situated at Steventon, some three and a half miles further west.

This small station now became the main railhead for the area, which also included Oxford; in fact timetables of the day informed travellers to change at Steventon for Oxford. They would then catch one of the many stagecoaches that travelled daily between the two points, the 10-mile drive taking about two hours. The importance of Steventon at this time was such that in 1842 alone some 77,000 passengers and 12,500 tons of goods passed through the station. It is also worth mentioning that between 21 July 1842 and 5 January 1843 the Station Superintendent's house at Steventon was also used for company board meetings, being situated approximately halfway between London and Bristol.

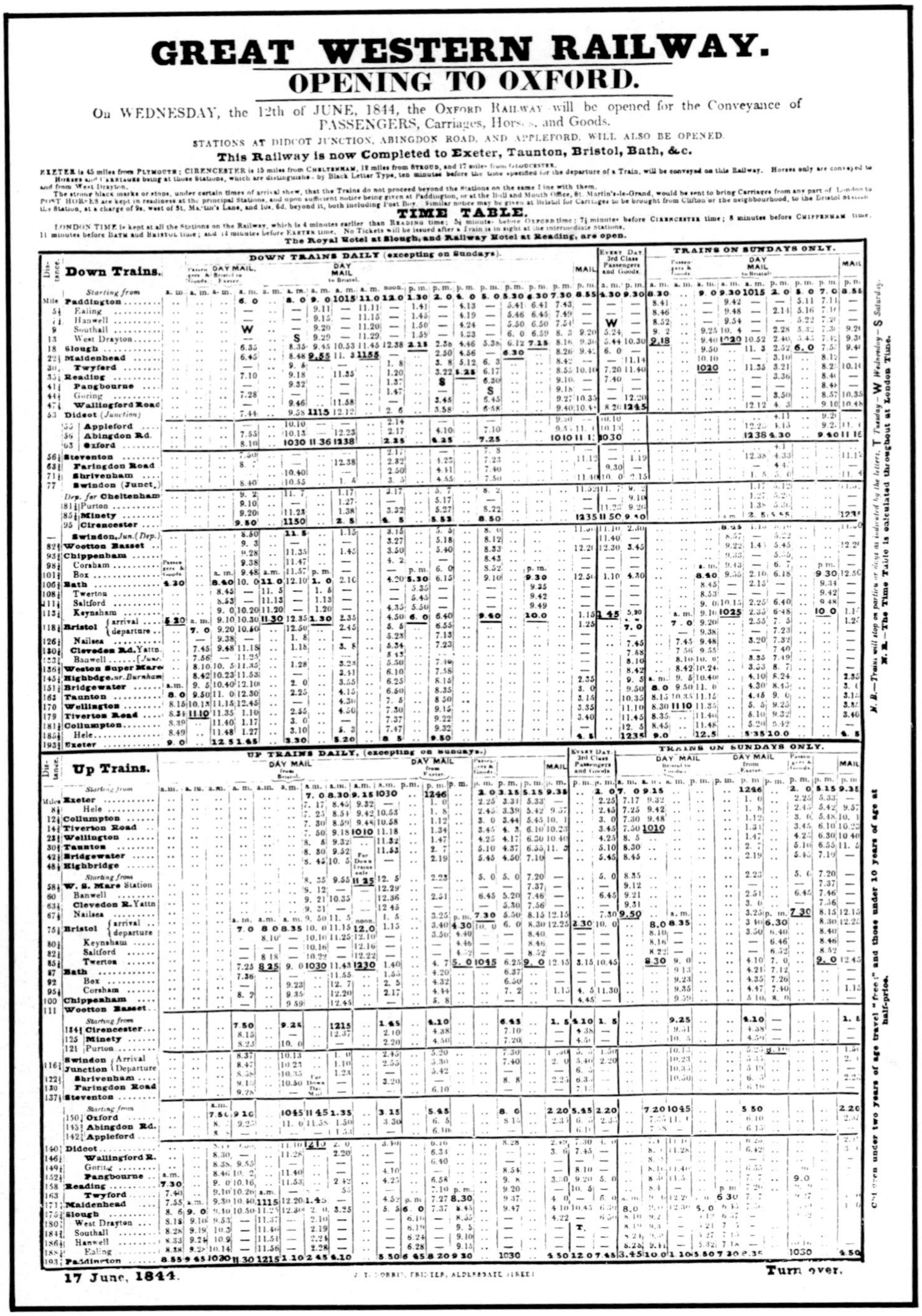
GREAT WESTERN RAILWAY.

OPENING TO OXFORD.

On WEDNESDAY, the 12th of JUNE, 1844, the OXFORD RAILWAY will be opened for the Conveyance of PASSENGERS, Carriages, Horses, and Goods.

STATIONS AT DIDCOT JUNCTION, ABINGDON ROAD, AND APPLEFORD, WILL ALSO BE OPENED.

This Railway is now Completed to Exeter, Taunton, Bristol, Bath, &c.

TIME TABLE.

The Royal Hotel at Slough, and Railway Hotel at Reading, are open.

Down Trains. / Up Trains.

17 June, 1844.

Turn over.

Left:
This timetable, issued for the opening of the Oxford Railway on 12 June 1844, shows Didcot Junction for the very first time. *David Castle collection*

Didcot continued to slumber along as a quiet Berkshire (it only became part of Oxfordshire in the mid-1970s) village until 12 June 1844, when a new junction station was opened to serve the Oxford Railway, which was also opened to traffic on the same date. A branch to Oxford had been proposed by the GWR in 1836, 1838, and again in 1840, and on each occasion the Oxford colleges, which were the major landowners, thwarted its attempts. In 1843 a fourth proposal was made by the newly formed Oxford Railway Co under the auspices of the GWR, and this time it was successful. The university authorities however still had a final say, for they insisted on a clause being inserted into the Act that did not allow university members below the status of an MA to travel on the railway, and proctors were to be given free access to the stations to check on this. Apparently this had arisen because of reports of large numbers of students travelling from Steventon to the races at Ascot.

The Act provided for a broad gauge branch some 9 miles 57 chains long from a junction at Didcot to land belonging to Brasenose College on the west side of the Abingdon turnpike road. The branch, along with new stations at Didcot Junction, Appleford, Abingdon Road (Culham) and Oxford, was duly opened for use on 12 June 1844.

The new station at Didcot, although small, was still quite impressive. Designed by Brunel, its four tracks were served by no less than five platforms, with each platform bay covered by a rather ornate canopy giving the station what was in effect an overall roof. The whole station structure, platforms included, was constructed of wood.

The new railway was to have a great impact, not just in terms of passenger usage but for the transport of all kinds of livestock. Prior to the arrival of the railway, livestock was moved on the hoof. A 1770 census of livestock movements across the Wallingford Bridge recorded 100,000 cattle, 250,000 sheep and hundreds of flocks of geese and turkeys. Once the railway arrived it was not long before much of this type of traffic was switched on to the rails.

The railway also provided many new jobs locally. The building of the main line, together with the Oxford branch, had brought some 300 extra men into the area and many were to stay on to work on the railway that they had helped to construct. Engines for the Oxford branch services were maintained at Didcot and had their own shed from 1844 until a new engine shed was built at Oxford. From 1850 the Didcot shed became a sub shed of Oxford, with engines being supplied by that depot. The usual allocation of Oxford engines to Didcot at this time was just six goods and one ballast engine. A new broad gauge shed had been built at Oxford during 1850 when the line was extended northwards by the Oxford and Rugby Railway Co. This undertaking had been formed in 1844 to construct a line from Oxford to connect with the London & North Western Railway (LNWR) at Rugby. However, by the time Fenny Compton had been reached, the company had passed into the hands of the GWR, which abandoned the Rugby portion and instead used the Birmingham & Oxford Junction Railway route from Fenny Compton to Birmingham. Trackwork from Oxford northwards was laid to mixed gauge and was opened through to Birmingham in 1852.

The increasing railway workforce at Didcot saw the need for extra housing and this was temporarily answered by the GWR which during 1854 built nine terraced houses close to the station at the top of Station Hill. The new development was known locally as Mount Pleasant or the Barracks. During the same year the Great Western Junction Hotel was built opposite the station forecourt. Many of its customers were wool buyers from the mills of Leeds and Bradford attending the nearby sheep sales at East Ilsley. Such was the general increase in trade that two further hotels were built adjacent to the station. During 1857 a corn exchange was established at Didcot, the building being situated just to the west of the station entrance. In July of the same year the small wooden broad gauge engine shed was replaced with a much more substantial brick-built structure, which will be described in detail later.

The population, many of whom were employed on the railway, continued to expand and more new housing was built to the southeast of the old village at

Northbourne by private contractors between 1868 and 1887. This area became known locally as Didcot New Town, and it was also known as the 'railwaymen's town' as so many of the residents were employed by the GWR. In 1904 the GWR also built a second row of employees' houses on the north side of station hill. These were the first houses in Didcot to be provided with gas which was supplied by the GWR from a small gas works situated in a yard alongside the engine shed.

Didcot East loop was opened on 22 December 1856, and on the same date mixed gauge services commenced between Oxford and Basingstoke. The line north of Oxford to Birmingham had been built as a mixed gauge line from the start, so, together with the new loop at Didcot, this now allowed standard gauge working from north to south, bypassing Didcot station, which at this time was still purely broad gauge. The first train to use the new connection was a standard gauge mixed goods service from Basingstoke to Birmingham. However, by 1 June 1863 mixed gauge track had been laid into the Oxford branch platforms, together with the adjoining yards. This now allowed for the first time standard gauge running into Didcot station. To facilitate the exchange of goods between the two gauges a wooden transfer shed was constructed to the west of the station adjacent to the Bristol main

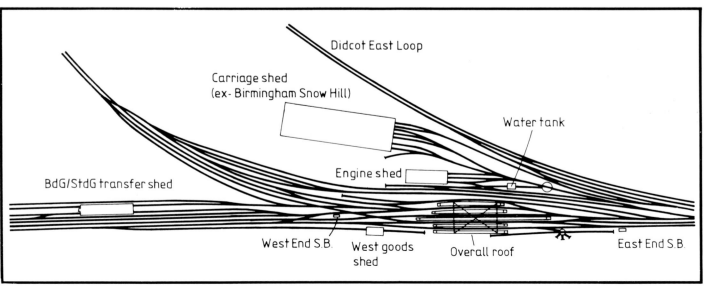

Didcot East Loop

Carriage shed
(ex- Birmingham Snow Hill)

Water tank

BdG/StdG transfer shed

Engine shed

West End S.B.

West goods shed

Overall roof

East End S.B.

line, and was opened for use during July 1863.

Didcot was now being served by fast broad gauge services to and from Paddington, Bristol and Exeter, together with the Oxford branch semi-fast and stopping trains. For several years from 1869 Didcot was also served by a slip coach that was detached from the evening express from Paddington to Birmingham. The procedure was to slip the coach on the approach to the East loop, the signalman would then quickly change the points once the express train had passed, diverting the slip coach, which was travelling under its own momentum, into the station, thus allowing its passengers to catch the stopping train to Swindon.

During 1871 the large wooden train shed that had served at Birmingham Snow Hill station since its opening in 1852, was dismantled and re-erected at Didcot. Here it saw use as a carriage shed until it was demolished during 1898. The shed, which contained under its roof seven rows of sidings, stood approximately on the site of the present-day steam depot. An interesting story has come to light regarding a small goods shed, that up to 1876 was situated at the west end of the station on the town side of the track. Apparently this shed was also adjacent to a local hostelry, in which it seems the workers were spending rather too much time. The GWR's solution to the problem, it appears, was to move the shed across the tracks into the station yard and well away from temptation.

By the 1860s standard gauge services were in the ascendancy, and on 1 November 1868 broad gauge services were withdrawn north of Oxford. Just four years later, on 25 November 1872, the last broad gauge service departed southwards from Oxford, the 7ft trackwork being removed almost immediately. From the same date mixed gauge lines were opened between Didcot and Swindon. Thus Didcot was now served by standard gauge trains to and from the Oxford branch and mixed gauge trains on the Paddington-Swindon route. From the summer of 1874 some standard gauge trains had commenced running between Didcot and Bristol via Trowbridge, although it must be said that at this time the main route to the West was still very much a broad gauge stronghold.

On 13 April 1882 the GWR's complete domination at Didcot came to an end with the opening of the first section of the Didcot, Newbury & Southampton Junction Railway (DNSJR). This ran from a new junction to the east of Didcot across the Berkshire Downs to the market town of Newbury, a distance of some 17½ miles. The DNSJR had been incorporated on 5 March 1873, to construct a line from Didcot southwards to connect with both the LSWR main line near Micheldever, and the Salisbury line at Whitchurch. However, by the time that the first sod of the northern section was cut at Newbury on 26 August 1879, not only had the company gained a new board of directors,

but these two connections had been abandoned. The Didcot-Newbury section was opened for traffic on 13 April 1882 and ran into a single bay platform that had been constructed at the east end of Didcot Junction station. In order to construct the bay the old signal cabin that stood at the east end of the down main platform was moved to a new position at the east end of the centre island platform. The initial service on the line comprised four passenger trains and one pick-up goods each way daily. Once again plans for completion of the southern section were changed and instead of running directly into Southampton via Winchester, Twyford and Chilworth, a decision was made to connect with the LSWR main line at Shawford, some two and a quarter miles south of Winchester. The section from Newbury to Shawford Junction was duly opened for traffic on 1 January 1891. Agreement had been reached between the DNS (the 'Junction' had been dropped from the title) and the GWR that the latter company would both staff and run the line, although the DNS continued to retain its independent status until it was absorbed by the GWR in 1923. Engines for the new line were provided from Didcot, with a new sub-shed being built at Winchester. This had an allocation of two to three engines; these were required for the engine changes

that took place at Winchester Cheesehill (later known as Chesil) station. The line provided a new shorter route from the north to the south and this was soon exploited, particularly by the Great Central Railway which from 1900 ran through carriages from Leicester to Southampton, a service which by 1903 had been extended through to Newcastle and Edinburgh, and which also included a restaurant car service.

Above:
This enlargement shows the interesting design detail of 'EAST END CABIN' here photographed on 20 May 1892. It was replaced by a new box at Didcot East Junction in 1934. *Author's collection*

Above right:
This east end view of the Provender Store, photographed on 24 April 1906, shows to good effect the power house and straw barn to the right of the main building. The large reservoir in the foreground held some 3,326,000gal of water; it supplied the nearby engine shed, and was for many years a favourite local fishing spot. The transfer shed can just be seen on the left of the picture. Note also the wagons filled with straw. *Author's collection*

Right:
The track layout and location of the Provender Store c1900. The station lies to the right of the reservoir.

The Horse Provender Store

Didcot was by now a junction of some importance and it was probably because of its central position within the system that the GWR established its Horse Provender Store here in 1884, on farmland just to the west of the station. This was the chief fodder store for the thousands of horses used by the company. Some stables and a horse recuperation field were also situated nearby, used mainly by horses from Paddington and Hockley. The main building was 202ft long, 49ft wide and 72ft high. Constructed of brick with a steel frame, its four floors were built of concrete to minimise the fire risk. The whole structure was flanked on each side by two towers each containing a water tank on the top. A

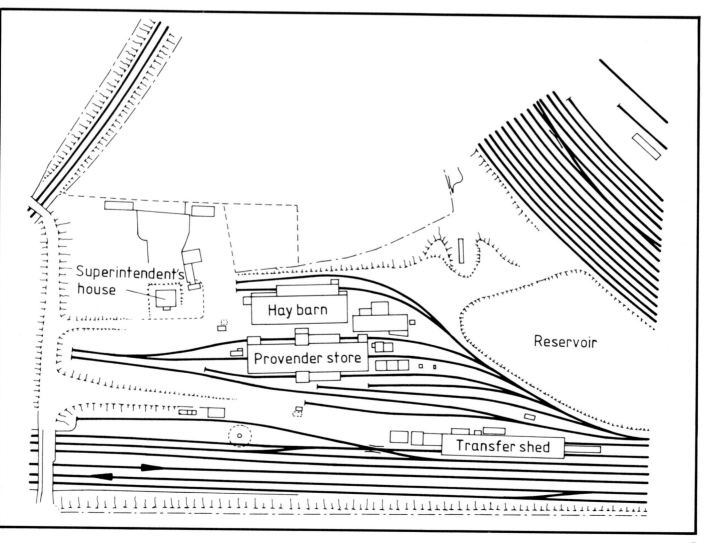

separate barn, which was capable of holding some 300 tons of straw, was added to the complex in 1900. At the turn of the century some 60 men were employed here, under the charge of the Superintendent Storekeeper who himself lived on site in a house provided by the company.

When opened the plant machinery was steam powered, but during 1901 electricity was installed in the shape of two 100hp dynamos, which were located in a new power house that was built alongside the barn. They supplied power to 16 separate motors within the main building and also to the water pumping station at Appleford a mile and a half away. This pumping station also supplied water to Didcot and East Hagbourne via the village reservoir.

Why was the store built at Didcot? Apart from its central position, the Provender Store was ideally placed in a predominately grain-growing area which ensured cheap and plentiful supplies. In fact it was because the railway became such a large buyer of grain locally, with the farmers selling direct to the company, that the corn exchange at Didcot went into liquidation during 1895 and was sub-

Below:
Standing in the triangle of lines to the west of Didcot was the Provender Store pictured here in 1910. The Superintendent's House can just be seen on the extreme left of the picture.
Author's collection

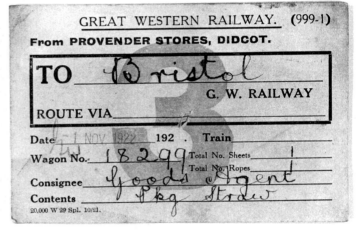

GREAT WESTERN RAILWAY. (999-1)
From PROVENDER STORES, DIDCOT.
TO *Bristol*
G. W. RAILWAY
ROUTE VIA
Date 1 NOV 1922 192 . Train
Wagon No. 18299 Total No. Sheets 1
Total No. Ropes
Consignee *Goods Agent*
Contents *Pkg Straw*
20,000 W 29 Spl. 10/21.

Above left:
The staff of the Provender Store 1914, the Store Manager, Mr Cullen is seated fifth from right, second row. This picture was kindly loaned to the author by his son who himself worked on the railway at Didcot until the 1930s. *H. D. Cullen*

Above:
A delivery ticket for one wagon of straw from the ex-Provender Store to Bristol, dated 1/11/22. *David Castle collection*

Left:
Shunting locomotive No 26 (Motor Rail & Tram Co 4178/20) at Swindon Works, 30 August 1953. *A. R. Carpenter*

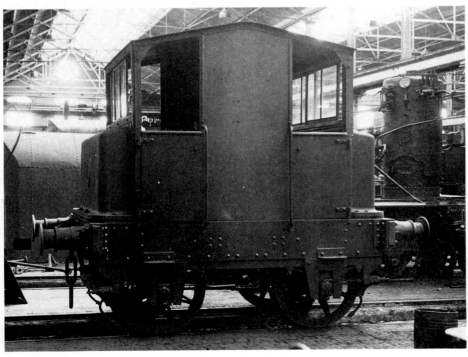

sequently closed. An example of the quantities of foodstuffs being used to mix the fodder can be gleaned from this October 1906 report which stated that the weekly quantities required were: '1,000 sacks of oats, 220 sacks of beans, 480 sacks of maize, 110 tons of hay, 16 tons of oat straw, 18 tons of bran and 40-50 tons of straw'. The mixture for a country horse was — oats 22½%, beans 10%, maize 20%, hay 41½% and oat straw 6%.

Right:
This interesting picture shows some of the station staff, including the station horse, at Didcot Junction about 1887.
David Castle collection

Below:
The 5pm service from Paddington to Plymouth stands in the down relief platform at Didcot Junction on a summer evening in 1890. Motive power is provided by two of Gooch's superb 8ft singles, *Great Western* and *Swallow* built in 1888 and 1871 respectively. Notice also the curve on what is today Platform 1; this was straightened soon after the removal of the broad gauge. *Great Western Trust*

Bottom:
This picture shows the aftermath of the fire at Didcot Junction on 11 March 1886. Rebuilding work had only been completed just a few months earlier. Notice also the large cast nameboard announcing 'DIDCOT JUNCTION'.
Courtesy Dr Malcolm Graham

London horses were supplied with 2½% more oats and a slightly lower amount of hay.

In 1927 the GWR obtained under Lot No 250 a four-wheel petrol mechanical locomotive specially for provender yard shunting work. Numbered 26 by the GWR, it continued to work at Didcot until 1959. It then lay out of use for some months before being withdrawn during July 1960. During World War 2, because of its close proximity to the ordnance depot, an anti-aircraft gun was installed on the roof of the main store building, but apparently saw little, if any, action.

As the use of horses on the system declined so did the importance of the Provender Store, until it was finally closed by the Western Region in 1953, surplus to requirements. Its use as a store continued however when it was let out to private firms for this purpose until 1963, after which it was closed completely. It languished in a derelict state for a further 13 years before it was finally demolished during April 1976. The only part of the complex to survive is the superintendent's house which nowadays stands alone in the vast Parkway car park.

On 15 February 1886 a new west curve some 35 chains in length was opened between Didcot North Junction and the Bristol main line at Foxhall Junction, so named because of its close proximity to the Foxhall Road bridge. It is probably worth mentioning at this point the origin of the usage of Foxhall. The name, it seems, is derived from the nearby farm, which at the time of James I was being used as a Royal hunting lodge. One of the King's favourite pastimes whilst in residence was fox-hunting, thus the house became known over the years as Fox Hall, the land and house eventually becoming Foxhall Farm. The farmhouse was purchased by the GWR and demolished in 1884 to make way for the new provender store and west curve, and a stained glass window from the house depicting a Scottish thistle and a Tudor rose was removed and subsequently displayed as a fire screen in the Directors' room at Paddington. In 1940 the stained glass suffered bomb damage during the Blitz and, after careful restoration of the remains into a single fragile panel, it was presented by the GWR to Reading Borough Council and was subsequently displayed from 1946 to 1980 in the old town hall at Reading. In 1981 it was handed back to Didcot Town Council and is nowadays displayed in the council chamber at the new civic hall. When the Army opened a barracks at Didcot in the 1920s, it used the name Vauxhall wrongly assuming this to be the older name, as both are shown on many early maps, although Vauxhall is in fact a much later derivative of Foxhall.

The west curve now provided a new direct connection between Oxford, Swindon and Bristol and through services were introduced almost immediately between Oxford and Weymouth. The small station at Didcot Junction now saw services arriving and departing from the north, south, east and west. This station was now proving quite inadequate for the increasing amount of traffic and between 1882 and 1885 it was extensively altered. Firstly the overall roof was removed and the three centre platforms were taken up. Alterations to the track layout then allowed a new centre island platform to be constructed, which served both the up and down lines, the down main platform was lengthened and new bays were provided at either end for Newbury and Swindon services. Within a few months of the completion of the rebuilding work disaster struck, when on Thursday 11 March 1886 (MacDermot states 1885 which is incorrect) a severe fire practically destroyed the new station with the downside platform and station entrance being particularly badly damaged. A local report of the fire in the *Jacksons Oxford Journal* of 13 March 1886 makes particularly interesting reading:

'Shortly before 1 o'clock on Thursday afternoon a fire broke out in one of the waiting rooms on the down platform of the GW station at Didcot Junction. The flames spread with such rapidity that in a very short time the refreshment rooms, offices etc were ablaze as well the platform itself. The wind was blowing the flames towards the middle platform and with a view to preventing them crossing the station and catching the buildings on the up platform, the middle one was partially torn up by the railway men, and even as it was the up express passing the station at about quarter to two had difficulty in getting through. The Oxford volunteer fire brigade were communicated with by telegraph and the steamer was promptly dispatched with several members of the brigade, and the immense quantity of water the engine was able to pour on the fire prevented it spreading, and was the means of saving a great deal of valuable property from destruction. The station which had been rebuilt had only very recently been finished, another will now have to be entirely built'.

Initially the fire was fought by the Harwell volunteer force; the Oxford brigade it seems received the call at the central station at 1.30pm and arrived at Didcot at 2.00pm (the distance by road is 10 miles). After the fire, rebuilding work was started almost immediately and by the end of the year the station was almost complete.

Above:
The last down broad gauge service, the 5pm Paddington to Plymouth is seen here passing Didcot on Friday 20 May 1892 hauled by the locomotive *Bulkeley*. Notice the standard gauge tracks into the Newbury bay, and East End signal cabin. *Author's collection*

Below:
This interesting view shows one of the early GWR Travelling Post Office vehicles, No 2085, at Didcot Junction c1890. It is attached to the 5.30am service from Paddington as the London and Bristol sorting carriage. The staff are seen posing for the photographer whilst the engine takes water. *Great Western Trust*

On Friday 20 May 1892 Didcot Junction saw its last broad gauge train to the west when at approximately 5.50pm the final service from Paddington to Plymouth passed through the station. The removal of the broad gauge provided the opportunity to carry out yet more improvements, with both the down main together with the down platform being realigned and straightened. The station layout at this time contained six platforms; the down main was Platform 1 and this also contained east and west bays numbered correspondingly 1 east and 1 west. Platform 2 was the down relief, Platform 3 up relief, and Platform 4, which was a single-sided platform, was used mainly for parcels

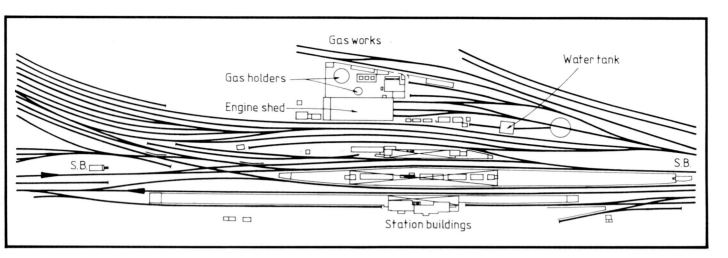

and local services between Didcot and Reading. It was probably at this time that the 'Junction' was dropped from the station name.

The whole layout at this time was controlled by five wooden signalboxes situated at Station East end, West end, North Junction, West Curve Junction and Foxhall Junction.

In July 1905 a new electric signalbox was installed at Didcot North Junction. This box was actually the first on the GWR to contain a power-operated interlocking frame, its signals and points being controlled from a 38-lever Siemens-Halske miniature frame. This new brick-built box replaced the two older mechanical boxes at North Junction and West Curve. It appears

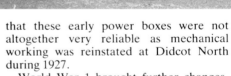

that these early power boxes were not altogether very reliable as mechanical working was reinstated at Didcot North during 1927.

World War 1 brought further changes, with the establishment, during 1914, of a large Army Ordnance Depot on land to the northwest of Didcot. This site was subsequently expanded over the years to over 1,000 acres, and contained some 30 miles of track within its boundaries. Within this large complex were stored all manner of military supplies from horseshoes to explosives. Such was the extent that it was said that the entire British Army could be equipped from Didcot within 48hr! During the 1920s the site was expanded once again when an aircraft maintenance factory was built to the west of the Ordnance Depot at nearby Milton. Interestingly in 1929 many Roman remains were found in the earthworks during the laying of a new siding into the Ordnance Depot.

By the 1930s over 1,200 civilians were employed at the Ordnance Depot alone, and in 1931 the Pimlico Clothing Co established its own small factory within the complex to manufacture service uniforms. World War 2 brought the busiest period ever to the depot with supplies being moved 24hr a day, seven days a week. By the mid-1950s its role was diminishing, and a decision was soon made to gradually run the depot down prior to closure. Much of its contents, together with a large number of its staff, were transferred to Bicester Central Ordnance Depot and during September 1964 Didcot Ordnance Depot was finally closed. The Didcot locomotive allocation over the years included the 0-6-0 tank engines specially fitted with spark arresting chimneys for Ordnance Depot shunting.

During the autumn of 1915 the King and Queen arrived at Didcot by Royal Train, from where they toured the area by car, after which they took dinner in the Royal Train which was parked behind Platform 4 and was therefore out of view from the public. The meal, rather interestingly, was prepared in the station restaurant and was then carried in hampers across the tracks to the dining car.

During World War 1 the goods yard adjacent to the station was enlarged, and new sidings were constructed between Chester Line Junction and North Junction. These became known as the Northern sidings, another group of three in the centre of the yard were known as the Dardanelles, probably because of their close proximity to the reservoir.

Between the wars the GWR undertook
many improvements to both its lines and
stations, and during 1928 it decided to
quadruple the main line between Didcot
and Wootton Bassett, which also involved
major alterations at Didcot station. The
line from Paddington to Didcot had been
quadrupled soon after the removal of the
broad gauge, the work finally being
finished during 1899. The new work at
Didcot was started during 1931 and
required the complete removal of both the
East End signalbox together with Platform 4. New relief lines were constructed
together with a new island platform on the
site of the old No 4. All existing platforms
were lengthened, with the Newbury bay
being upgraded to include an engine
run-round loop, together with a new
livestock loading bank. The addition of the
new platform now gave Didcot a total of
seven, numbered thus: east bay 1, west bay
2, down main 3, up main 4, down relief 5,
up relief 6, Oxford branch and parcels 7.
At East Junction a new 150-lever signalbox
was opened during February 1932,
replacing both East End and East Junction
boxes. A new box was also provided at
Foxhall Junction, once again being a direct
replacement for an older box. These boxes
were unusually constructed using a steel

girder frame filled with large concrete
slabs, although they still retained the
standard GWR signalbox design. The
whole area was also resignalled at the same
time. The new layout completely trans-
formed Didcot and really for the first time
allowed unrestricted high-speed running
on both up and down main lines. One such
service to exploit the new layout was the
GWR's crack train the 'Cheltenham Flyer',
which from September 1932 had its
Swindon-Paddington schedule cut to just
65min. The high speed potential of the

newly quadrupled and realigned track had
been exploited just a few months earlier
when on 6 June 1932 the 'Flyer', hauled by
'Castle' No 5006 *Tregenna Castle* ran the
77.3 miles in just 56min 47sec, at an
average speed of 81.7mph. Census figures
for 1932 show there were 480 employees at
Didcot and some 275 trains of all types
passing through daily. The locomotive
department was not forgotten in the
modernisation work with the old 1857
engine shed being replaced by a new
four-road shed built on the site of the old

carriage sidings. This shed is described in detail in the next chapter. World War 2 brought much activity to the area, as Didcot became one of the major hubs of the war effort on the GWR. Several major alterations were undertaken locally, notably the doubling of 20 miles of the DNS between Didcot and Woodhay and the construction during April 1941 of a new 16-siding yard at Moreton (to the east of Didcot). Many new goods loops were constructed locally, including extending

Above:
The exterior of Didcot East Junction signalbox pictured shortly after its erection on 2 December 1931. Note its unusual construction using concrete slabs. *Author's collection*

Below:
Didcot station and locomotive depot c1950.

the up loop from Didcot North Junction through to the new yard at Moreton.

The doubling of the DNS was started on

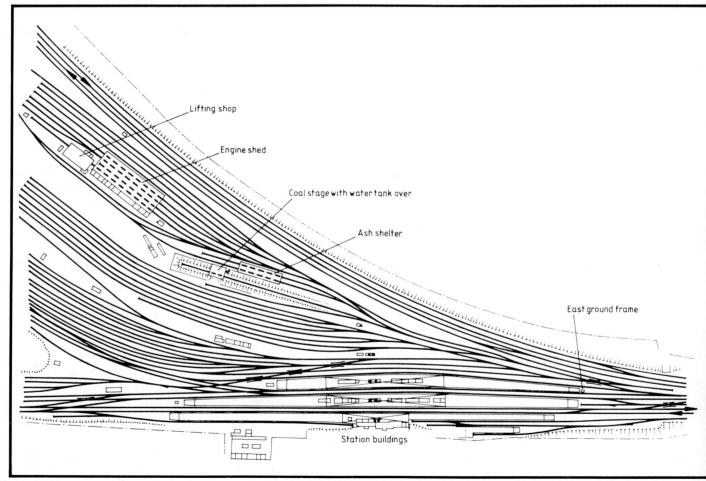

Lifting shop

Engine shed

Coal stage with water tank over

Ash shelter

East ground frame

Station buildings

4 August 1942, and from that date all passenger services were withdrawn to allow total possession of the line. The work was carried out by contractors McAlpine aided by a number of Italian prisoners of war. The work was finished and services restored on 8 March 1943. It is worth remembering that whilst it was the original intention of the DNS way back in 1882 to build a double track line; it was to take some 60 years and a war to finally achieve it! South of Newbury many extra passing loops were installed and suddenly a line that had seen only minimal traffic since its opening took on new importance as a major north-south through route. It was not long before it was being used to full capacity, particularly in the build-up to D-Day. Contemporary reports state that in the 12 months prior to 6 June 1944 some 16,000 military trains alone travelled southwards, an astonishing number, if correct. Certainly many hospital trains also used the route running from the south to the large military hospital at Holton near Wheatley. Didcot itself was becoming so busy at this time that goods trains would sometimes be stuck in sidings and goods loops nose-to-tail for days on end. It was not unknown for some crews to be relieved at the end of their turns without actually having moved at all!

A new residential staff hostel, the first of its kind on the GWR, was opened at Didcot on 3 May 1944. It was constructed by the Ministry of Works on land to the southeast of the station. Built for the

wartime welfare of the staff it contained a large canteen, and some 100 sleeping cubicles. Reading, writing and recreation rooms were also provided within what was, at the time, the largest building of its type on the railway.

Once the war was over the railways gradually got back to normal. Nationalisation came and went seemingly having little effect on the Western Region, which of course was still regarded as the GWR by many of its employees. During the 1950s the railways went through a sort of Indian summer with many new services being introduced, and increasing numbers of passengers using them. Didcot probably saw its busiest time ever in terms of passenger train movements. By 1952, staff

figures had risen to 610, and there were some 350 trains passing through the station daily. During the 1950s the Western Region introduced many new named expresses, and these, together with some

Above:
Didcot c1957 with 'Mogul' No 5397 at Platform 5, and 'Hall' No 4918 *Dartington Hall* at Platform 6. *John Edwards*

Below:
The east end of the station has always been a good location for viewing workings over the East Curve. In this 1962 picture No 7007 *Great Western* hurries towards London with the up 'Cathedrals Express', passing on the left Didcot locomotive depot. *Tony Simpkins*

of the longer-established named services, brought back memories of the old GWR. Eight of these passed through Didcot daily; they were as follows: the 'South Wales Pullman', the 'Red Dragon', 'Pembroke Coast Express', the 'Capitals United', the 'Merchant Venturer', 'Cheltenham Spa Express', the 'Bristolian' and the 'Cathedrals Express' (via East curve).

The DNS, for so long the domain of GWR motive power, also saw changes during this time. In 1950 the southern half of the line passed to the control of the Southern Region and on 8 June 1953 the small sub-shed at Winchester was closed. Engine changing at Winchester now ceased and Southern and Western Region engines now worked over the whole of the route. Particularly interesting visitors to Didcot at this time were the LSWR 'T9' class engines

Above:
The view looking west from Platform 5 in 1959 shows the down platform starting signals and also Chester Line Junction with the Oxford line diverging away to the right. In the centre of the picture stands Didcot West End signalbox.
Author's collection

Below:
During the 1950s Southern engines appeared almost daily on through workings from Southampton and Eastleigh via the Didcot, Newbury and Southampton route. Seen here at Didcot on 13 July 1959 is ex-LSWR 'T9' class No 30313 with the 3.38pm service to Eastleigh; this also conveyed through coaches from Oxford. *H. Burchell*

Above:
Cardiff Canton-based 'Castle' No 5021 *Whittington Castle* passes Milton, just west of Didcot, with a down train on 22 September 1961. Withdrawn a year later after covering 1,446,936 miles in service, this locomotive was cut up by J. Cashmore of Newport, Gwent, but 'Castles' No 5029 *Nunney Castle* and No 5051 *Earl Bathurst* survive at the Didcot Railway Centre. *Michael Mensing*

Below:
GWR '57XX' class 0-6-0PT No 3665 basks in the sun at Didcot on 22 September 1961. Two '57XXs' are preserved at Didcot Railway Centre: Nos 3650 and 3738. *Michael Mensing*

Above:
Shunting at Didcot on 26 September 1959 is Hawksworth 0-6-0PT No 1502; this engine was allocated to Didcot from 1953 until it was withdrawn in January 1961.
Dr John Coiley

Left:
This picture shows the last multiple slip working in the British Isles taking place on 7 June 1960 at Didcot Foxhall Junction, from the 07.00 Weston-super-Mare-Paddington. *Dr John Coiley*

on the through services from Eastleigh and Southampton.

Unfortunately the 1950s also saw Didcot's worst railway accident when at approximately 1.13pm on 22 November 1955 a Treherbert to Paddington excursion was derailed at speed on Milton embankment, a mile and a half to the west of the station. Due to track repairs to the up main, the train hauled by 'Britannia' Pacific No 70026 *Polar Star* was switched to the up goods loop at Milton. The driver it appears was quite unaware of the diversion and subsequent speed restriction. There were also visibility problems when these engines ran on the Western Region which meant he also did not see the signal until it was too late. The train approached the up

goods loop at more than 50mph, and the subsequent violent change of direction derailed the engine which, together with most of its train, plummeted down the adjacent embankment. Unfortunately 11 passengers were killed and 157 injured. The coaches were easily cleared but the 94-ton locomotive proved to be quite a problem, and was not finally moved until 4 December when it was taken out through the Ordnance Depot site.

On 15 June 1959 the Wallingford branch was closed to passengers. This small branch was opened by the Wallingford and Watlington Railway Co on 2 July 1866. Built as a standard gauge line it ran from Wallingford Road station, later named Moulsford, to a terminus at Wallingford, a

distance of some three and a quarter miles. Original plans to build the line right through to Watlington never materialised. For many years Didcot had supplied the branch engine, in the early days a '517' class 0-4-2T and in later years a '48XX' class 0-4-2T.

The 1960s brought many changes to the railway locally with the introduction of diesel traction to many of the main line workings and also diesel multiple-units (DMUs) on to the suburban services. The start of the decade saw an end to slip coach working at Didcot, when on 7 June 1960 the last regular multiple slip took place from the 07.00 Weston-super-Mare to Paddington service. Unfortunately the modernisation of the 1960s also brought with it yet more line closures. With passenger numbers dwindling, local services over the southern half of the DNS were withdrawn from 7 March 1960. The writing was on the wall for the northern section and it was to be no real surprise when local passenger services were also withdrawn between Didcot and Newbury from 10 September 1962. The line continued to be used as an important through goods route, with up to 11 trains a day in each direction, many of these being oil trains to the Midlands from the large refinery at Fawley. Regular diversions also saw cross-country passenger trains such as

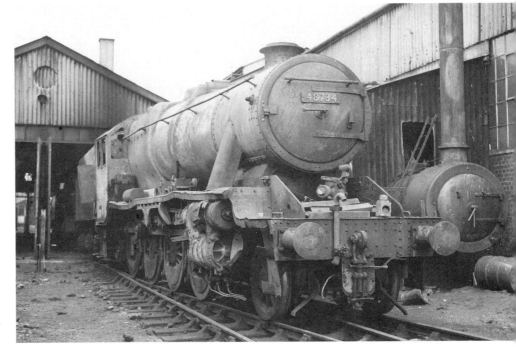

the 'Pines Express' use the route. These it seems were not enough to justify the maintenance costs of the line and on 10 August 1964 the DNS was closed completely, with services being diverted over the longer route via Basingstoke and Reading.

Only five days after closure a major accident occurred at Didcot North Junc-

Left:
'Hall' class 4-6-0 No 4939 *Littleton Hall* gets underway from Steventon with the 12.25pm Swindon-Didcot train on 22 September 1961. This locomotive was based at Didcot shed at the time. It did not survive, but No 4942 *Maindy Hall* and No 5900 *Hinderton Hall* are preserved at Didcot along with 'Modified Hall' No 6998 *Burton Agnes Hall*. *Michael Mensing*

Below left:
'94XX' class 0-6-0PT No 8430 moves off from Moreton Cutting sidings with an up freight, 22 September 1961. No 9466 of this class, preserved at Quainton Road, is a regular visitor to Didcot Railway Centre. *Michael Mensing*

Below:
The 'Bristol Pullman' — the 12.45pm departure from Paddington — storms through Milton composed of a Metropolitan-Cammell 2,000hp eight-car set finished in the striking 'Nanking blue'. *Michael Mensing*

Bottom:
Standard 350hp shunter D3964 stands at the head of a rake of mixed wagons, including a GWR shunter's truck, alongside Platform 7 at Didcot, 22 September 1961. The locomotive, now numbered 08792, is based at Laira. *Michael Mensing*

tion, to a service that only a week previously was using the DNS route. On 14 August 1964 at approximately 2.17am a down train of 48 full petrol tankers, travelling from Fawley to Bromford Bridge behind a pair of Type 3 (now Class 33) diesels, was struck by a light steam engine. The collision occurred approximately half-way along the train, and one of the petrol tanks was unfortunately ruptured. This resulted in a severe fire that soon engulfed many of the tankers, but quick thinking by the railway staff on hand saw the first 20 of these uncoupled and taken away to safety. Because of the inaccessible position of the train the fire services were severely hampered and only after many hours was the blaze brought under control. The light engine, LMS '8F' No 48734, was severely damaged and withdrawn. An adjacent footbridge was also damaged by the incredible heat and was subsequently replaced by a redundant footbridge from Challow. Stopping services were withdrawn between Didcot and Swindon on 7 December 1964, with all intermediate stations being closed from the same date. Thus within two short years both the east and west bays at Didcot were closed, and the remaining platforms renumbered with the down main becoming Platform 1, up main 2, down relief 3, up relief 4 and the Oxford/parcels 5. The local Swindon stoppers had been used for many years as running-in turns for recently outshopped engines from the works, and motive power on what were normally only two coach

trains could produce anything from a '22XX' 0-6-0 to a 'King'. Yet another closure that took place in this same year was the marshalling yard at Moreton to the east of Didcot and during May 1965 the up goods loop from North Junction to Moreton yard was also removed. By now steam was becoming the exception rather than the rule and on 14 June 1965 Didcot engine shed was closed to steam. On 31 December steam working officially ceased on the Western Region with the closure of Oxford shed, but Southern Region steam workings through to Banbury continued to use the East loop at Didcot until August of the following year.

Considerable alterations took place on the signalling front with multiple-aspect signalling (MAS) being introduced at Didcot on 17 May 1965. On this same date the remaining four signalboxes at Didcot West End, East, North and Foxhall Junctions together with the box at Moreton were closed and control was switched to the new power box at Reading. On 27 September 1967 the 09.45 service from Paddington to Bristol was derailed at speed at Didcot West; as with the Milton accident of 1955 the driver was unfamiliar with the

Below:
No 47064 on the 12.50 service from Paddington to Oxford here overtakes No 47360 on a down tanker train at Moreton cutting. The overgrown site of the wartime marshalling yard which was closed during 1964 can be seen in the background. *Brian Morrison*

Above:
No 6026 *King John* approaches Didcot with the 11.55am stopping service from Swindon. The local services between these two points were regularly used as ex-works running in turns, hence the appearance of a 'King'. *T. E. Williams*

Right:
'Warship' class No 867 *Zenith* is seen here standing on the up relief line at Didcot West on 7 October 1971. The newly constructed power station already dominates the skyline. *N. E. Preedy*

Below:
Prototype IC125 set 252.001 is seen here at Didcot on 12 January 1975, whilst carrying out dipped rail joint tests in preparation for the introduction of High Speed Train services. *Barry J. Nicolle*

route. The nine-coach train, hauled by 'Warship' class D853 *Thruster*, was running at speed on the down relief line. Passing through Didcot it hit the junction from the relief to the down main at Foxhall at a speed estimated at between 70-75mph. Incredibly the engine and the first five coaches remained on the tracks, the rear four coaches were however derailed, one of which included amongst its passengers noted railway author O. S. Nock; luckily for such a high speed derailment only one person was killed and 23 were injured.

Between 1973 and 1975 extensive track and signalling work was undertaken on the Paddington-Bristol main line in preparation for the introduction of the proposed IC125 high speed trains. On

Top left:
The final Mogul allocated to Didcot shed, No 6309, is seen on 20 September 1964, after withdrawal. *A. Doyle*

Left:
'Warship' class No D859 *Vanquisher* leaves Didcot with an up parcels train on 12 March 1966. *Steve Boorne*

Below left:
A Hereford-Paddington service passes Didcot via the East loop hauled by 'Warship' No 853 *Thruster* in the spring of 1971. This was the locomotive involved in the high-speed derailment at Didcot on 27 September 1967. *Author*

Above:
The spirit of the 19th century GWR is conjured up by this view of the replica 4-2-2 *Iron Duke* preparing to leave the resited Transfer Shed. The complexities of mixed-gauge track are apparent. *M. Howse*

Below:
Once the saddle tank was as ubiquitous on the GWR as the pannier tank became in later years. The last class of saddle tanks to be constructed by the GWR was the '1361' class. No 1363 is preserved at Didcot Railway Centre and is seen here in 1983. *Author*

13 October 1973 Richs siding was closed. This small siding was situated between the east end of the station and the Newbury line. It was opened on 14 July 1888 and served what was in effect Didcot's first industrial estate which contained both coal and general hauliers' sidings. In later years an oil depot together with a small wagon repair shop were also established here.

During 1975 high speed tests were carried out using the gas turbine APT; the alterations to the track were obviously successful with a speed of 150mph being recorded near Didcot on one of the runs.

Diesel-powered IC125s were gradually introduced on to the Bristol and South Wales routes during 1976, completely transforming the services in both speed and comfort. It now became possible to reach Paddington (53¼ miles) including a Read-ing stop in just 45min and Bristol (65¼ miles) in 59min. This had the effect of making the Didcot area prime commuting country, and to this end British Rail decided to promote Didcot as the local railhead for the area (just as Steventon had been way back in 1841). The site of the Provender Store was cleared and during 1984 a large car park was established on the site. The station received considerable attention with the construction of a new entrance lobby and booking hall, and a travel centre was also incorporated within the building. The down main platform was extensively rebuilt with the provision of a new public waiting room together with a new building for station administration. The down main platform was also length-ened to allow access to a footbridge that was installed across the Bristol line giving passenger access to the car park which is now one of the largest on the Western Region, holding almost 1,000 vehicles. Unfortunately during the refurbishing work to the other platforms extensive wood rot was found in the Platform 5 waiting room, which resulted in it being demolished and replaced with a prefabri-cated structure. To finish off the improve-ments the station was renamed Didcot

Top:
A quiet Sunday evening at Didcot sees a Swansea-Paddington service about to arrive at Didcot Parkway, unusually on the up relief line because of engineering work on both the up and down main. The large expanse of the car park can be seen behind the IC125 unit. *Author*

Above left:
The fine frontage to Didcot Parkway is shown to good effect in this photograph, incorporated into the design is a ticket office for the Railway Centre (left). *Autho*

Left:
The spacious booking hall at Didcot Parkway incorporates automatic entrance doors, a snack bar and Travel Centre.
Author

Parkway on 29 July 1985, not without some local dissent.

Today Didcot is still a busy junction, used daily by some 400 trains of all types, and the East avoiding line carries much cross-country traffic, both passenger and freight. The West loop is now used by several stone trains and by up to 18 merry-go-round (MGR) coal trains daily, delivering some 4 million tons of coal annually to the CEGB power station from East Midlands pits. The power station stands on the site of the old ordnance depot. Building work was started in 1965, and the first generator was ready to operate in September 1970. The power station today covers an area of some 585 acres and has four 500MW generating units in operation, which incidentally, can generate enough power for 10 cities the size of nearby Oxford. The remainder of the Ordnance Depot land together with the defunct aircraft repair factory at Milton has been used for a new trading estate and inland port by Lansdown Estates Milton Ltd. The whole complex was fully opened during the summer of 1981. The main transit shed covers an area of some 97,000sq ft and contains under its roof a customs bonded area. The rail-linked warehouses are currently served by a daily Speedlink service, with wagons being delivered from Didcot yard by an '08' class pilot.

Didcot Parkway is an InterCity station.

Top right:
Still in good external condition is the Provender Store Superintendent's House that now stands alone at the entrance to the Parkway car park. *Author*

Right:
No 47345 leaves CEGB Didcot and returns to the Midlands to have its empty wagons replenished with yet more coal for the power station. April 1982. *Author*

Below:
This overall view shows No 47620 *Windsor Castle*, on a Bristol-Paddington service, entering Platform 4 at Didcot Parkway on 5 May 1988. Notice the refurbished and raised face on the down main platform, and also the reduction in length of Platform 3. *Author*

Above:
'2884' class 2-8-0 No 3822, repainted in wartime black livery, stands outside the Engine Shed at Didcot in August 1988.
M. Howse

Below:
The sumptuous interior of Collett Ocean Saloon *Queen Mary*, No 9112 of 1931. *Author*

Above:
Collett TPO Brake Stowage Van No 814 stands by the Engine Shed. It was constructed in 1940 to diagram L23. *Author*

Below:
Collett Third No 5952 of 1935 stands on the ex-Midland Railway traverser from Derby, which was rebuilt at Didcot in 1977. *M. Howse*

The station manager currently has a staff of 22, and although the loco depot has long since closed, there are still 50 drivers based here. The main line services through Didcot are now worked almost exclusively by IC125s, although DMU and locomotive-hauled services still form the bulk of the Oxford line traffic. A new sprinter service was introduced during 1988 between Didcot and Hereford, and this is supplemented by an evening IC125 service between Paddington and Hereford that calls at Didcot at 17.49. There are currently 11 services daily from Didcot to Bristol, 34 to Oxford and 31 to Paddington. Passenger usage has risen considerably in recent years, current figures showing some 592,000 passenger journeys a year originating at Didcot.

For many years the goods yard adjacent to the station was little used, in fact closure and lifting had been mooted on many occasions. In 1987 Didcot became a main distribution depot for Speedlink concentrated house coal services, the activity being centred on the main station yard which is now designated as Didcot Terminal Complex. Each day many coal trains arrive and after being re-sorted in the yard, depart to such destinations as Fratton, Temple Mills, Westbury and Aylesbury. Motive power for these services is provided by Class 37 locomotives supplied by Cardiff Canton depot, which are stabled between turns in the station yard. Pilot duties are performed by a Reading-based Class 08 shunter. It seems that services to and from Didcot will continue to grow in the future, for the old centre sidings, unused for many years, are still being retained for wagon storage.

That then is the story, albeit a brief one, of the railways at Didcot.

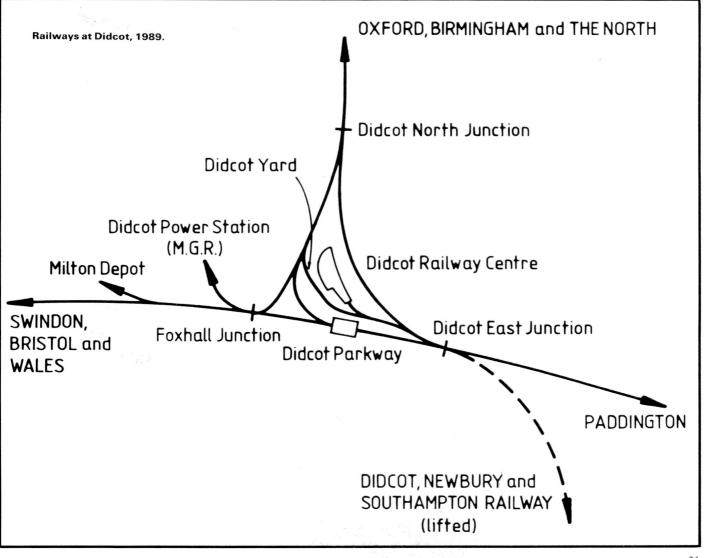

Railways at Didcot, 1989.

OXFORD, BIRMINGHAM and THE NORTH

Didcot North Junction

Didcot Yard

Didcot Power Station
(M.G.R.)

Didcot Railway Centre

Milton Depot

SWINDON,
BRISTOL and
WALES

Foxhall Junction

Didcot Parkway

Didcot East Junction

PADDINGTON

DIDCOT, NEWBURY and
SOUTHAMPTON RAILWAY
(lifted)

Above:
The National Railway Museum's recreation of *Iron Duke* is seen in action on the Centre's broad gauge demonstration track. *M. Howse*

Right:
It attracts! *Hinderton Hall* enthrals a young admirer with the magic of steam.
Brian Higgins

The Locomotive Depots 1844-1965

Locomotive servicing facilities have been provided at Didcot in one form or another since 1844. The first engine shed was opened during June 1844 to house the broad gauge engines working on the Oxford Railway. It was constructed of wood and contained a single road, with two further sidings alongside and access was achieved via a 40ft turntable. This shed continued to be used until July 1857, when it was demolished and replaced by a new larger building situated on the same site. Built of brick with a timber gabled roof covered in slates, the new shed measured approximately 130ft by 50ft. Initially built as a two-road broad gauge shed, it was converted to mixed gauge during 1863 at which time a third road was added by the addition of a lean-to section tagged on to the east side of the existing building. In the yard alongside stood the shed coal stage. As before, the original 40ft turntable controlled entry to the shed roads and also

the siding which ran under the shed water tower. This was quite an impressive structure built of brick which supported a 35,000gal water tank. In later years a small gas works was established on land adjacent to the shed, and this supplied gas to both the station and, from 1904, the railway cottages at the top of Station Hill. In July 1850 the GWR had opened a new engine shed at Oxford, from which date Didcot became its sub-shed, and it appears that it remained so until at least 1863, as the Gooch registers for this year still show engines working at Didcot to be part of Oxford's allocation. After this date it appears that Didcot once again had its own allocation, which comprised a varied selection of both broad and standard gauge engines.

The opening of the DNS in 1882 saw the allocation increase with extra motive power for the new line. Examples of both 'Queen' and 'River' classes saw regular use

on the line at this time, supplemented by both Armstrong and 'Dean Goods' 0-6-0 types. By the turn of the century the allocation stood at 33 with the majority comprising 0-6-0 and 0-4-2 tank classes, many of which had been working at Didcot well before the removal of the broad gauge.

In 1911 the 40ft turntable was replaced with a 65ft example, at a new location in the yard to the northeast of the shed. During 1918 the GWR set up a system of locomotive depot divisions, with Didcot being placed in the London division and coded DID.

By the 1920s some of the older engines had been replaced with newer types

Below:
This picture shows to good effect the brick construction of the 1857 engine shed at Didcot, as 'Dean Goods' No 2530 moves slowly past on the up goods avoiding line in June 1929. *E. Eggleton*

although the shed now had several 'Barnum' 2-4-0 engines dating from the 1880s in its allocation. Special mention must be made of locomotive No 2190. This Brecon & Merthyr 0-6-0ST arrived at Didcot during April 1930. Built in 1881 it was taken into GWR stock in October 1922, and was the oldest surviving Brecon & Merthyr engine. During March 1930 it was overhauled at Swindon and fitted with a spark arresting chimney for Didcot Ordnance Depot working, which it continued to do until it was withdrawn in May 1934, having amassed 1,043,500 miles in its lifetime.

In June 1932, under the Government Loans Act of 1929 the shed was replaced once again. The new building was constructed only a short distance away on land that once was the site of the old carriage shed and for a few days at least, until the changeover was complete, both sheds were in use simultaneously. It was not long however before the old brick shed was demolished to make way for new goods and carriage sidings.

The new shed, Didcot's third, was built by Holcombe & Sons of Cardiff. It measured some 210ft long and 67ft wide, and its four roads could accommodate between 16 and 24 engines according to

Below:
Didcot locomotive yard, pictured in April 1960, with No 4959 *Purley Hall* and in the background '9F' No 92002. *Author*

Right:
This view shows the back of the locomotive shed at Didcot in April 1960, with an assortment of engines that include Nos 5330 and 3751. *Author*

their dimensions. A new coal stage with a 74,250gal overhead water tank was situated at the London end of the running shed. Repairs were taken care of by the provision of a lifting shop which was situated at the rear of the running shed and contained a 50-ton engine hoist, together with associated machinery such as lathes and drilling machines. Alongside the lifting shop stood a small shed that contained the locomotive wash-out boiler. Offices, stores and enginemen's rooms ran along the southwest side of the main running shed. The 65ft turntable was situated some distance away in the sidings behind the lifting shop, and was almost certainly the same turntable that had been installed during 1911, for its position within the site was unchanged. Although such an up-to-date depot, engine coaling was still undertaken by hand, using ½-ton iron tubs. Labour was obviously still cheap in those days! The shed opened with an allocation of some 45 engines, which included for the first time a 4-6-0 in the shape of No 4902 *Aldenham Hall*. Gradually the old guard of 'Dean Goods', 'Dukes' and 'Bulldogs' were replaced by 'Halls', 'Moguls' and '28XXs'. Little change took place at the depot until the

advent of World War 2 when the allocation was considerably increased by the addition of many engines on loan, notably LMS and 'USA' 2-8-0s. During 1940 the ash roads were covered by a large corrugated iron shelter to shield the ash glow from enemy aircraft.

Once the war was over Didcot settled down to normal working. However, during 1946 proposals were put in hand to convert the shed for the use of oil-fired loco-motives, but apart from some preliminary work the project was abandoned. Nationalisation seemingly had little effect on the shed other than a change of coding from DID to 81E.

With its engines now sporting their new shed code the 1950s saw many of the older classes disappear from Didcot. One of these was Didcot's last 'Duke', No 9083 *Comet* which was withdrawn in December 1950. Dübs 2-4-0 No 1334 of 1894 vintage was withdrawn in October 1952 and the shed's last 'Dean Goods' No 2532 was withdrawn in May 1954. This latter class had been associated with Didcot since before the turn of the century. It seemed that the reallocation to Oxford in Septem-

ber 1953 of 'Dukedog' No 9015 signalled the end of 4-4-0s at Didcot, but this was not to be, for during 1957 *City of Truro* was taken out of retirement and allocated to Didcot for working enthusiasts' specials. It earned its keep working ordinary passen-ger trains over the DNS line.

The widespread closures of the 1960s together with the gradual removal of steam traction saw the role of the shed diminish

and rather surprisingly during 1962 a start was made on refurbishing the shed roof, together with the provision of new smoke extraction hoods. Eventually someone must have realised what a waste of money this was, but not before three of the rows had been replaced was the decision taken to stop.

In 1961 there were only four pannier tanks at the depot, Didcot's only outside-

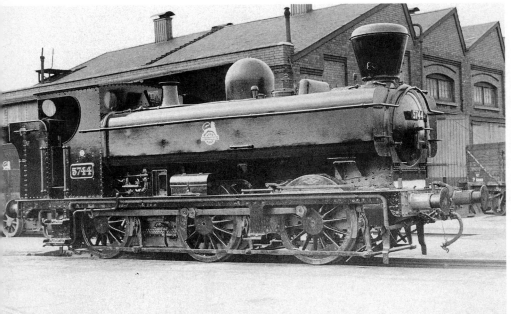

Left:
0-6-0PT No 5744, allocated to Didcot for shunting at the Ordnance Depot, is seen at Swindon in November 1955. *G. Wheeler*

in the yards. In October 1964 Didcot's last pannier tank, No 8720 was withdrawn and the remaining months of 1964 also saw the end of many other longstanding classes at Didcot. During September, Mogul No 6309 was withdrawn, October saw 0-6-0 No 2221 allocated away to Banbury, and finally November brought the withdrawal of Didcot's last 2-8-0 No 2893. An era was rapidly coming to an end and by the turn of the year the allocation stood at just 17 engines, four '61XXs', 10 'Halls' and three 'Manors', the 'Manors' arriving from Reading during January. The end eventually came on 14 June 1965 when the depot was closed to steam, its remaining engines either going for scrap or moving up the line to Oxford and Gloucester to work for a few more months. The shed continued to be used until 1969 as a diesel signing-on point, the only obvious change from steam days being the removal of the turntable, and the sight at weekends of Class 47s, 'Hymeks' and 'Warships' standing under the still sooty shed roof. Unlike many redundant steam depots however, Didcot survived the bulldozer to become the eventual home of the Great Western Society.

cylinder 0-6-0, No 1502, was withdrawn in January. The allocation was however supplemented by several members of the '61XX' class and, for the first time, by three Hawksworth 'Counties', although these only lasted until October 1962.

During the last few years, steam was joined by diesel when three Standard Class 08 350hp shunters allocated to Oxford were outstabled at Didcot for work

Below:
Hawksworth '15XX' class 0-6-0PT No 1502, a Didcot engine for most of its career up to withdrawal in January 1961. *F. W. Day*

The Great Western Society

I suppose if you mention the name Didcot today a fair number of people may remark about the power station, others may mention Didcot Railway Centre. I would like to think nowadays the latter answer would be in the majority, for since 1967 Didcot has been the home of the Great Western Society, which, in the ensuing years has built up a magnificent collection of GWR artefacts ranging quite literally from pen nibs to steam locomotives. The 16-acre site is now firmly established as one of the major tourist attractions in the area and is currently visited by over 100,000 people each year, many of whom are non-enthusiasts but are still interested enough in both the old GWR and the excellent day out that Didcot Railway Centre now provides.

All of this started with the dream of four schoolboys, way back in 1961, of saving just one small tank engine from the scrapyard. Little did they know then just exactly what they were starting, for today the Great Western Society owns or administers some 24 steam locomotives, three diesel locomotives, 43 coaches, 37 wagons and four rail-mounted cranes. The vast majority of items are of GWR origin and this is undoubtedly the largest single collection of GWR rolling stock anywhere.

The first tentative steps towards the formation of the Great Western Society were made during 1961 when an advert was placed in the *Railway Magazine* inviting subscriptions towards the possible purchase of a '48XX' class 0-4-2T locomotive.

Below:
The early days of the Great Western Society with No 6998 *Burton Agnes Hall* at Totnes Quay in 1966. 'Dreadnought' 70ft coach can just be seen in the background.
Great Western Society

Left:
No 6106 is seen here approaching Didcot with a special ecs working from Kensington and Taplow on 4 November 1966. The two Pullman cars were delivered to Oxford before No 6106 proceeded to Didcot Depot, thus becoming the first Society engine to take up residence.
Patrick Russell

Below:
The first public open day was held at Didcot on 20 September 1969. Seen here on this date are from left to right 0-4-0ST *Bonnie Prince Charlie*, Wantage Tramway No 5, GW diesel railcar No 4, 2-6-2T 6106 and 70ft Dreadnought coach No 3299. Note the unprotected East avoiding line.
Frank Dumbleton

With interest being forthcoming from the advert, the 4800 Preservation Society was formed. Within a short space of time it was decided by the then committee to effect a change of name, and by the time the inaugural meeting was held at Slough on 4 May 1962, the name had been changed to the Great Western Preservation Society. A year later at the meeting on 4 June 1963, a decision was taken to drop the word 'Preservation' from the title, and thus the Great Western Society was born. In June 1962 the first issue of the Great Western Preservation Society newsletter was published, but by the time the third issue was produced the society change of name also led to a change in the name of the news-sheet, and for issue No 4 (March 1963) the name *Great Western Echo* was adopted. The *Echo* has continued to

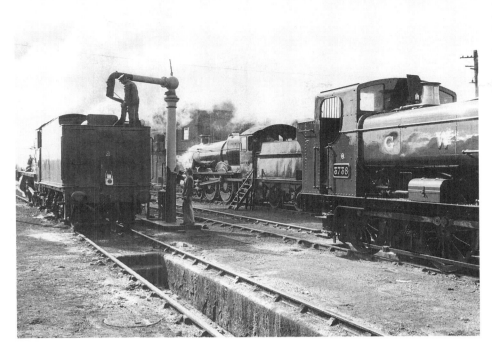

Left:
The atmosphere of a Great Western shed yard is recreated once again at Didcot, as No 6998 *Burton Agnes Hall*, No 7808 *Cookham Manor* and No 3738 are prepared for another open day. *Author*

Below:
The vintage train 1975 style, seen near Wyre Piddle, Worcestershire en route from Didcot to Hereford on 14 June 1975, hauled by No 7808 *Cookham Manor* and No 6998 *Burton Agnes Hall*. *Les Nixon*

society member from storage at Laira. The society was now growing fast and by the end of 1964 had doubled its membership, owned two engines and had just successfully completed the purchase of auto-coach No 231.

During 1965 the society was big enough to form local branch support groups and these were set up in the South-West, London, Reading, Swindon, Bristol and South Wales. During the same year a fund was started to save a two-cylinder 4-6-0 from the cutter's torch, with eventually the decision being taken to go for a 'Modified Hall' in the shape of No 6998 *Burton Agnes Hall*. This engine was in good all-round condition and had ended up at that last bastion of steam on the Western Region, Oxford. The engine had the honour, if that is the word, of working the very last official steam-hauled passenger service on the Western Region when at 14.10 on 3 January 1966 it worked the Bournemouth to York service between Oxford and Ban-

provide news and well researched articles on anything Great Western. It is now published four times a year and the 100th edition was reached during 1987.

By the autumn of 1963 adequate funds had been donated to effect the purchase of an 0-4-2T. Two engines came in for consideration, Nos 1450 and 1466 and eventually a decision was made to go for the latter. In February 1964 the engine was duly purchased from Taunton, where it had been in store, and moved to a contractor's yard at Totnes. This location was chosen because of its close proximity to the Dart Valley Railway where at this time it was envisaged it would run. It was joined here in August 1964 by 0-6-0ST No 1363 that had been purchased by a

bury. The locomotive by this time was devoid of its nameplates so local boiler-smith Len Cross manufactured a set of wooden ones that the engine duly carried on its last run. Within a few days of this event the society's bid of £2,500 was accepted by BR and the engine was saved.

Mention must be made of the first major open day. Organised by the Reading group it was held at Taplow in September 1965, attracting over 2,000 visitors, who were able to view No 4079 *Pendennis Castle* along with various other BR exhibits. The exercise was carried out once again on 17 September 1966 with the addition of Nos 6106 and 7808 *Cookham Manor* which arrived with a railtour from the Midlands. To everyone's amazement over 6,000 people turned up, even though there was still a fair amount of steam left on BR at this time. It proved that there was great interest in both steam open days and things Great Western. By the end of 1966 the society had amassed several locomotives, coaches, and other stock which were stored as far apart as Taplow, Totnes and Gloucester. It was now becoming clear that a single location would have to be found for this rapidly expanding collection. The formation of the Dart Valley Railway Association in November 1965 to administer the running of that railway had signalled for the eventual removal of society stock away from Totnes. Negotiations with BR on the finding of a possible site came to fruition in 1967 when the society were offered the closed steam depot at Didcot, still being used at this time by BR as a signing-on and stabling point. A final open day was held at Taplow in September 1967, after which the society prepared to move to its new home. The stock from Taplow was moved on 4 November 1967, with No 6106 being the first society engine to arrive. This was followed on 2 December 1967 by the stock from Totnes which moved *en bloc* to Didcot under its own steam, so to speak, as Nos 1466 and 6998 together hauled the various other items of rolling stock all the way from Plymouth to Didcot unaided. The only items of stock not to make the journey were locomotive No 1363 and coach No 7372 which were moved to the South-West group's site at Bodmin and No 1369 which stayed to work on the Dart Valley Railway. With the arrival at Didcot of the Totnes stock on the evening of 2 December 1967 the story of Didcot Railway Centre had begun.

Didcot Railway Centre

Once the society had established itself at Didcot thoughts turned to the successful open days at Taplow and the need to generate some income. On 15 April 1968 the society successfully operated an autotrain on the Wallingford branch in connection with the local carnival.

A members' open day was held at Didcot in June 1968, and arrangements were made with BR (which still used the

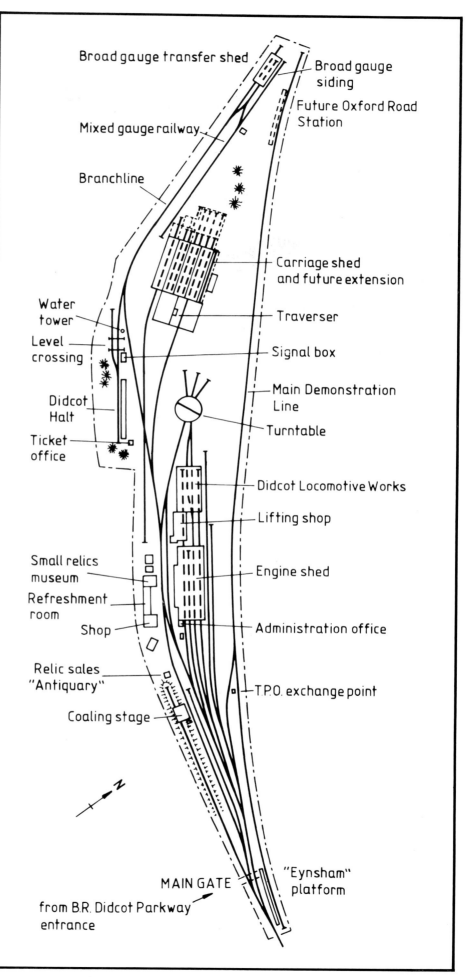

Broad gauge transfer shed — Broad gauge siding

Future Oxford Road Station

Mixed gauge railway

Branchline

Carriage shed and future extension

Water tower — Traverser

Level crossing — Signal box

Didcot Halt — Main Demonstration Line

Ticket office — Turntable

Small relics museum — Didcot Locomotive Works

Refreshment room — Lifting shop

Shop — Engine shed

Relic sales "Antiquary" — Administration office

Coaling stage — T.P.O. exchange point

N

MAIN GATE — "Eynsham" platform

from B.R. Didcot Parkway entrance

depot) to hold a public open day on 20 September 1969. This proved to be a great success with some 4,500 people turning up to see Nos 1466, 6106 and 0-4-0ST *Bonnie Prince Charlie* in steam. The formula was thus set for many more public open days. These early open days were amazing affairs with the public wandering everywhere, for at this time there was no dividing fence between the depot and the BR tracks. Later open days saw the area roped off and patrolled by stewards. Catering for the many visitors to the first open days was provided from a marquee erected by members, water for hot beverages being supplied by hosepipe. By the autumn of 1969 BR finally vacated the shed, the society was now on its own. One of the first tasks was to fence the perimeter of the site (which at this time only extended as far as the turntable pit) with a 6ft high fence. The small lifting shop at the back of the shed was used at this time for storing *Pendennis Castle*, and it was not until this locomotive left the site during 1972 that the society was able to use the building. During the same year a 520yd long demonstration line was laid; known as No 8 road, train rides were given from a temporary platform constructed of railway sleepers that was situated at the Oxford end of the line. In 1984 a concrete platform from Eynsham near Oxford was erected at the Didcot end of the demonstration line, thus at last allowing the 'temporary' wooden platform to be removed.

During 1974 the society had successfully

negotiated to extend the site as far as Didcot North Junction, now giving it an effective area of some 16 acres, and as before the whole perimeter was fenced. It was also at this time that the wartime cover over the ash road was found to be in a rather unsafe condition and for safety reasons was removed.

So much stock was now arriving on site that the area around the engine shed was becoming increasingly congested. This was relieved during 1977 with the construction of a large carriage shed measuring some 120ft by 140ft on the newly acquired land behind the engine shed. This now gave the society some 960ft of covered accommodation over seven tracks, together with a fully enclosed restoration bay. It was the

Above left:
This is one postbox that the GPO unfortunately does not collect from. It stands outside the small relics museum at Didcot. *Author*

Above:
Assistant Curator Peter Rance and Museum Steward Ken Miles are seen here discussing another new exhibit for the small relics museum. *Author*

Below:
A ticket for the first all-vintage train. *Author's collection*

society's first major piece of building work on site. Entry to the shed is effected via a Midland Railway carriage traverser from Derby Works; built in 1890 it became

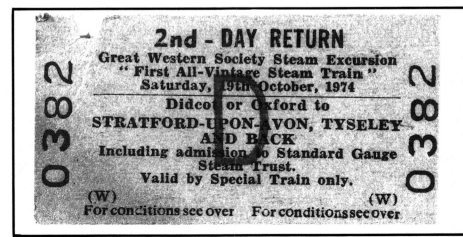

42

Above:
During 1986 broad gauge trains ran once again at Didcot in the form of the replica locomotive *Iron Duke*, on loan for the season from the National Railway Museum. It is shown here on 26 May 1986 with its two replica passenger vehicles, giving rides over the broad gauge demonstration line. *Melville Holley*

Right:
More potatoes sir? Happy diners enjoy the comfort of Super Saloon No 9118 *Princess Elizabeth*. The society owns three of these ex-Ocean Liner Saloons, two of which see regular usage throughout the year for Sunday luncheon and Wine and Dine evenings. *Author*

redundant in 1974, and was purchased by the society and subsequently installed at Didcot during 1977. During its latter years at Derby the tractor unit was electrically powered, but for use at Didcot the tractor unit was rebuilt and is nowadays powered by a Leyland Metro engine and automatic transmission unit. Several of the carriages that were now being kept in the new shed had previously been restored to running order inside the steam depot, and on 19 October 1974 these were used to form the first all-vintage steam train. This ran between Didcot, Stratford-upon-Avon and Tyseley, hauled by No 7808 *Cookham Manor* and No 6998 *Burton Agnes Hall* together with seven fully restored GWR coaches. The society's first railtour from Didcot had been run two years earlier on 1 October 1972 using *Burton Agnes Hall*

and a mixture of both society and BR stock. Unfortunately the high cost of maintaining the vintage train to main line standards saw it make its final run on the 'Sunset' railtour on 26 January 1980, hauled by newly restored No 5051 *Drysll-wyn Castle*.

The amount of manpower needed to maintain the vintage train could now be channelled towards the site generally. In the mid-1970s the society had published a 10-year plan for Didcot; included in it was much of what we can see at Didcot today, and there is no doubt that it was a great success. During 1977 another vital piece of equipment, in the form of a 70ft turntable was obtained from Southampton New Docks. The original 65ft GWR turntable had surprisingly been removed by BR soon after the shed was closed to steam traction. Preparatory work and installation of the new turntable took several months with the old pit having to be enlarged and relined with new facing bricks, being officially opened on Easter Sunday 1978 by disc jockey David Hamilton, together with engine No 7808 *Cookham Manor*. The new

turntable had been built in 1935 by Ransomes & Rapier Ltd for the Southern Railway, and its installation now allowed the society to turn the largest of engines.

Open days continued to attract many members of the general public to the site, and gradually facilities were improved and upgraded. In 1973 a small refreshment room was opened adjacent to the engine

shed, and this has subsequently been extended to include a staff restaurant. It is nowadays flanked on each side by a bookshop and a small relics museum. These two buildings are constructed in brick, and were opened during 1982, the latter on 29 August by television presenter John Craven. The small relics museum was a much needed amenity, for the society's

Above:
This picture taken in July 1980 shows Didcot Halt under construction. The halt in true Great Western fashion is almost entirely built from wooden railway sleepers. *Brian Higgins*

collection of small items had expanded rapidly as the society became more widely known and donations of material increased. Within the walls of this small building is a veritable Aladdin's cave of GWR memorabilia, probably the largest and most comprehensive collection anywhere in the world. The museum today is administered by the Great Western Trust, a separate body of society members set up to ensure the safe keeping of the valuable artifacts.

One aspect of the old company that was missing on site was some form of broad

Below:
The unusual sight of No 6106 entering Didcot Halt on a dull April day in 1988. Because of its size this engine is quite a rare performer on the branch, being generally used at Didcot on the main demonstration line. *Author*

gauge exhibition. The Taunton group solved this problem when in 1978 they found a large quantity of broad gauge rail on the site of the Westleigh Mineral Railway at Burlescombe in Devon. This was subsequently removed to Didcot and gradually relaid by the Taunton group at the Oxford end of the Centre. It was decided to relay the track as mixed gauge and the first section was completed and duly opened on 27 September 1980, when the standard gauge portion of the track was used for the first time by the visiting replica locomotive *Rocket*. By 1986 the broad gauge demonstration line was finished and once again saw broad gauge trains when, for the whole of the summer season, the *Iron Duke* replica on loan from the National Railway Museum worked passenger services over the track. It was a fitting tribute to the Taunton group whose time and effort had made the impossible into a reality. Alongside the broad gauge display stands the transfer shed. This large wooden

structure originally stood adjacent to the Bristol main line on land now used for the Parkway car park. Built in 1863 it was used for the interchange of goods and parcels

Above left:
Standing at the entrance to Didcot Halt is the beautifully restored booking office from Welford Park on the Lambourn Valley line. It is this type of restoration project that makes the centre such an interesting place to visit. *Author*

Left:
On most weekends the visitor will find society members working on various projects around the site. On this occasion a small group are seen laying a new track spur, connecting the new locomotive works to the turntable. *Author*

Above:
One of the major attractions on the branch demonstration line is the signalbox from Radstock North, together with a fully operational double gate level crossing that is operated from within the box, both being installed by the Bristol group of the society. Also in the picture can be seen the small water tank that once stood at Bodmin. *Author*

Right:
In 1986 the society staged a re-enactment, using the transfer shed, of the scramble from the broad to the narrow gauge Birmingham train at Gloucester, as depicted in the *Illustrated London News* of 6 June 1845. The engine is the replica *Iron Duke* and the coach Toplight No 3755.
Frank Dumbleton

traffic between the broad and narrow gauges. The shed survived *in situ* until 1979 when it was given to the society by BR. It was dismantled using manpower services labour and subsequently re-erected in the Railway Centre where it will be used as a station on the demonstration branch line. Construction of this ¼ mile-long branch

was started way back in 1979 and it was partially opened during 1981. Work on the branch is still continuing today, much of it on the signalling side, with the reconstruction of Frome North signalbox at the Oxford end. The main attraction on the branch is the Didcot Halt and Radstock box complex. The halt represents a typical

GWR utility station of the 1930s, and has been created using redundant buildings and fittings from around the Western Region. Entrance is effected via the booking office rescued from Welford Park on the long-closed Lambourn Valley branch. Incidentally this small building when first erected on site served on open days as the small relics museum. The branch platform itself is constructed of wood and contains an original pagoda waiting shelter from Stockcross and Bagnor Halt, once again from the Lambourn Valley line. In case the reader thinks this type of structure is now unique, one only has to travel a mile and a half along the Oxford branch to Appleford to see an almost identical halt still in use. Completing the scene is the signalbox from Radstock North. This was purchased and erected by the Bristol group of the society, being officially commissioned for use during 1985. The box now controls all signals and pointwork at the Didcot Halt

DIDCOT
LOCOMOTIVE WORKS
OPENED BY COUNCILLOR BRYN DUGGAN
CHAIRMAN OF OXFORDSHIRE
COUNTY COUNCIL
SUNDAY 24TH APRIL 1988.

Above:
The plaque commemorating the opening of Didcot Locomotive Works. *Author*

Below:
The interior of auto-coach No 190 is now nearing completion after years of painstaking restoration work. When finished it will give the society two fully operational auto-coaches for use on the branch demonstration line. *Author*

end of the branch, as well as a pair of level crossing gates. The installation of these took nearly three years to complete, and was probably the biggest and most complicated civil engineering job undertaken by the Bristol group on the site to date. The group is currently rebuilding a second box that once stood at Frome

North. When this project is complete it will mean that the branch line will be fully signalled throughout. The transfer shed will then form the Northern station on the branch and when finally finished will be named Burlescombe.

Even with all of these activities it is still the steam locomotive that continues to attract the interest of the enthusiast and public alike. The need to provide and maintain a running fleet is an expensive and time-consuming business. For many years the restoration and repair work was undertaken in the running shed and lifting shop. Although successful this was not a very satisfactory state of affairs, so in 1987 a new locomotive works measuring 118ft by 60ft was constructed at the back of the old lifting shop. It was officially opened on

24 April 1988 by the Chairman of the Oxfordshire County Council, Councillor Bryn Duggan, himself a former Didcot railwayman. The new works, which will eventually contain a wheeldrop, is large enough to undertake all the Didcot locomotive repairs, with perhaps some capacity for repairs to outside locomotives as well.

Having taken care of the locomotive department, the society has now turned its eye to the carriage and wagon department and the construction of a large extension to the carriage shed. When finished in a few years time it will give some 2,000ft of covered storage space, thus ensuring that all the carriage stock will be kept under cover. Unlike the locomotives, carriages are constructed mainly of wood and therefore suffer much more serious damage when exposed to the elements. The new carriage shed and extended restoration shop will enable much more long term restoration work to be carried out throughout the year, irrespective of outside weather conditions.

A very popular feature at the Steam Centre are the Sunday lunches and Wine and Dine evenings, using the two 'Ocean Liner' coaches, and many societies, groups and families have relived the days of the luxury train in these historic vehicles. Although the society is still primarily run by volunteers the increasing popularity of the Centre has seen the need to employ two full-time members of staff in the form of a General Manager and a Marketing

Right:
A good eye and a steady hand are needed to produce the high standard of finish so evident on the society's rolling stock. Here Andy Williams from the Severn Valley Railway applies the finishing touch to 'City' stock brake third No 3755.
Frank Dumbleton

Below:
The Ocean Liner Saloons see extensive use at Didcot for Sunday luncheon and Wine and Dine evenings throughout the year. Here the catering staff pose for a photograph prior to another luncheon sitting. These coaches are currently out of use for refurbishing. *Author*

Executive. Extended daily opening during 1988 has meant that these have also been joined by several part-time staff to look after the museum, bookshop and ticket office.

Long term plans should see the completion of the Oxford Road station project at the North end of the Centre. This entails the rebuilding of Heyford station, donated by BR, previously dismantled and removed by members and currently stored as various piles of numbered stones at the Oxford end of the Centre. This station will be served by the No 8 main demonstration line that was extended for a further 340yd to the Oxford Road end during 1986. The society is very aware of the need to adequately landscape the site, and to this end much tree and shrub planting has been undertaken with examples of ash, birch, blackthorn, field maple, hawthorn, holly and rowan now firmly established. Adjac-

ent to the Oxford Road site is a wild area, which contains several rare species of plants.

Newly arrived on site is the Firefly Project; this is situated inside the new locomotive works, and the gradual reconstruction of this replica broad gauge locomotive will certainly provide an interesting extra attraction for Didcot workers and visitors alike.

Surprisingly there is still much that the

society would like to do. A new museum, library and study centre are urgently needed, as is a larger book and souvenir shop, and the increasing numbers of visitors may see the need for extended refreshment facilities. The next 10 years should see many changes, but whatever happens one thing is sure, future generations will still be able to sample the delights of the old Great Western Railway at Didcot Railway Centre.

Appendix — Didcot Stock List

GWR Locomotives at Didcot Railway Centre: Building and Allocation Details

822 *The Earl* (2ft 6in gauge)
0-6-0T. Built Beyer Peacock 1902 for the Welshpool & Llanfair Light Railway. Numbered 1 by this company, renumbered 822 by GWR 1922. Locomotive placed in store at Oswestry 11/56. Withdrawn 8/61 and sold to the Welshpool & Llanfair Preservation Society 7/62. After many years on display at various railway museums moved to Didcot in early 1989.

1338
0-4-0ST. Built Kitson & Co Leeds 1898 for Cardiff Railway. Cost £1,361, taken into GWR stock September 1922.
Allocations: 9/22 Cardiff (East Moors), 3/26 Cardiff (Docks), 7/43 Taunton, 6/60 Swansea East Dock. Withdrawn 30/9/63, sold to 1338 Fund 28/4/64 and placed on display at Bleadon and Uphill where it languished for many years before arriving at Didcot 8/87.
Mileage on withdrawal 353,985.

1340 *Trojan*
0-4-0ST. Built Avonside Engine Co, Bristol 1897. Cost £605 sold to Alexandra Docks & Railway Co April 1903.
Allocations: 4/03 Pill (Newport), 4/23 Cardiff (East Moors), 7/23 Tondu, 8/23 East Moors, 10/23 Cardiff Docks, 6/24 Radyr, 6/26 Cardiff (Docks), 2/27 Radyr, 2/28 Cathays, 4/28 Old Oak Common, 9/28 Cardiff (Docks), 11/29 Radyr, 12/29 Severn Tunnel Junction, 2/30 Radyr, 2/31 Cathays, 7/32 Swindon. Withdrawn 6/34, sold to Victoria Colliery, Wellington, Staffs. Eventually sold to Alders Papermills, Tamworth, from where it was purchased and taken to Didcot 3/68.
Mileage on withdrawal 134,848.

1363
Churchward '1361' class 0-6-0ST. Built Swindon 6/1910. Cost £1,182.
Allocations: 9/10 St Blazey, 1/11 Plymouth, 1/12 Looe, 2/12 Moorswater, 3/12 Plymouth, 9/16 St Blazey, 11/20 Plymouth, 2/44 Newton Abbot, 3/44 Plymouth, 3/45 Taunton, 4/45 Plymouth. Withdrawn 11/62, purchased 8/64 and subsequently kept at Totnes, before

moving to Bodmin 5/1969 and finally to Didcot 10/77.
Mileage on withdrawal 892,346.

1466
Collett '48XX' class 0-4-2T. Built Swindon 2/1936 as 4866, renumbered 11/46. Cost £2,247.
Allocations: 3/36 Newton Abbot, 3/38 Exeter, 6/38 Newton Abbot, 11/39 St Blazey, 9/40 Newton Abbot, 12/40 St Blazey, 7/41 Newton Abbot, 10/45 Exeter, 11/45 Newton Abbot, 5/61 Exeter, 10/63 Taunton. Withdrawn 12/63 and sold to Great Western Society 2/64 and kept at Totnes until 12/67 when it moved to Didcot.
Mileage on withdrawal 728,230.

3650
Collett '57XX' class 0-6-0PT. Built Swindon 12/1939. Cost £2,844.
Allocations: 1/40 Tyseley, 10/53 Bristol (Bath Road), 12/53 Radyr, 1/54 Cardiff (East Dock), 5/55 Abercynon, 5/58 Bristol (St Philips Marsh), 10/61 Neath. Withdrawn 10/63 and sold to Stephenson Clarke Fuels Ltd, Gwaun Cae Gurwen. Purchased by the Great Western Society and stored at Bulmers, Hereford 10/69, moved to Didcot 5/71.
Mileage on withdrawal 493,103.

3738
Collett '57XX' class 0-6-0PT. Built Swindon 9/1937. Cost £2,614.
Allocations: 10/37 Old Oak Common, 10/49 Slough, 10/50 Reading, 9/60 Tondu, 8/64 Radyr, 5/65 Cardiff (East Dock). Withdrawn 8/65, sold to Woodham Bros, Barry. Purchased for Great Western Society and moved to Didcot 4/74.
Mileage on 28/12/63, 497,440.

3822
Collett '2884' class 2-8-0. Built Swindon 4/1940. Cost £4,545.
Allocations: 7/40 Llanelly, 12/41 Neath, 10/42 Cardiff (Canton), 2/47 Pontypool Road, 6/60 Severn Tunnel Junction, 9/62 Aberdare, 12/62 Neath, 10/63 Cardiff (East Dock). Withdrawn 1/64 and sold to Woodham Bros, Barry. Purchased by Great Western Society and moved to Didcot 5/76.
Mileage on 28/12/63, 649,765.

4144
Collett '5101' class 2-6-2T. Built Swindon 9/1946. Cost £7,175.
Allocations: 10/46 Tondu, 2/47 Severn Tunnel Junction, 6/57 Tondu, 12/62 Severn Tunnel Junction. Withdrawn 6/65 and sold to Woodham Bros, Barry. Purchased by Great Western Society and moved to Didcot 4/74.
Mileage on 28/12/63, 312,520.

4942 *Maindy Hall*
Collett 'Hall' class 4-6-0. Built Swindon 7/1929. Cost £4,375.
Allocations: 8/29 Newton Abbot, 9/30 Fishguard, 4/32 Landore, 7/32 Fishguard, 9/33 Llanelly, 6/35 Carmarthen, 1/37 Weymouth, 11/38 Westbury, 11/40 Bristol (St Philips Marsh), 4/46 Bristol (Bath Road), 7/55 Banbury, 6/60 Exeter, 11/60 St Philips Marsh, 7/62 Canton, 9/62 East Dock, 10/62 Didcot. Withdrawn 12/63 and sold to Woodham Bros, Barry. Purchased by the Great Western Society and moved to Didcot 4/74.
Mileage on withdrawal 1,331,714.

5029 *Nunney Castle*
Collett 'Castle' class 4-6-0. Built Swindon 5/1934. Cost £4,955.
Allocations: 5/34 Old Oak Common, 3/58 Worcester, 5/59 Newton Abbot, 11/59 Laira, 12/62 Cardiff (East Dock). Withdrawn 12/63 and sold to Woodham Bros, Barry. Purchased for the Great Western Society and moved to Didcot 5/76.
Mileage on 28/12/63, 1,523,415.

5051 *Earl Bathurst*
Collett 'Castle' class 4-6-0. Built Swindon 5/1936 as *Drysllwyn Castle*, renamed 8/37. Cost £4,848.
Allocations: 5/36 Landore, 6/61 Neath, 2/63 Llanelly. Withdrawn 5/63 and sold to Woodham Bros, Barry. Purchased by a Great Western Society member and moved to Didcot 2/70.
Mileage on withdrawal 1,316,659.

5322
Churchward '43XX' class 2-6-0. Built Swindon 8/1917. Cost £3,312. Renumbered 8322 1/28, 5322 6/44.
Allocations: 8/17 ROD France, 8/19 Worcester, 10/19 Chester, 7/22 St Philips Marsh, 5/25 Weymouth, 11/26 Bristol

(St Philips Marsh), 11/29 Weymouth, 1/33 Cardiff (Canton), 8/36 Oxley, 7/44 Didcot, 6/45 Swindon, 2/53 Oxford, 4/53 Tyseley, 10/54 Oxford, 8/56 Didcot, 12/58 Reading, 6/59 Tyseley, 9/59 Pontypool Road. Withdrawn 4/64 and sold to Woodham Bros, Barry. Purchased for the Great Western Society and moved to Caerphilly, finally being moved to Didcot 9/73.
Mileage on 28/12/63, 1,355,622.

5572
Collett '4575' class 2-6-2T. Built Swindon 3/1929. Cost £3,578.
Allocations: 3/29 Exeter, 10/33 Kidderminster, 9/35 Westbury, 8/36 Yeovil, 9/36 Westbury, 1/41 Bristol (Bath Road), 7/53 Cathays, 1/55 Pontypool Road, 4/56 Laira, 3/58 Laira, 10/60 St Blazey, 5/61 Laira. Withdrawn 4/62 and sold to Woodham Bros, Barry. Purchased by the Great Western Society and stored at Taunton 8/71, finally being moved to Didcot 7/77.
Mileage on withdrawal 928,789.

5900 *Hinderton Hall*
Collett 'Hall' class 4-6-0. Built Swindon 3/1931. Cost £4,341.
Allocations: 4/31 Paddington, 5/31 Worcester, 6/31 Hereford, 8/33 Carmarthen, 1/35 Swindon, 5/36 Bristol (Bath Road), 5/37 Bristol (St Philips Marsh), 3/38 Westbury, 12/39 Swindon, 6/44 Bristol (St Philips Marsh), 11/46 Westbury, 7/53 Tyseley, 12/55 Oxley, 10/62 Bristol (St Philips Marsh). Withdrawn 12/63 and sold to Woodham Bros, Barry. Purchased by the Great Western Society and moved to Didcot 7/71.
Mileage on withdrawal 1,200,282.

6106
Collett '61XX' class 2-6-2T. Built Swindon 5/1931. Cost £4,160.

Allocations: 6/31 Slough, 8/33 Old Oak Common, 11/35 Penzance, 12/35 Didcot, 1/44 Slough, 8/53 Oxford, 10/62 Slough, 3/63 Reading, 1/64 Swindon, 7/64 Worcester, 1/65 Southall, 9/65 Oxford. Withdrawn 12/65 and sold in working order to a society member. Stored initially at Taplow, No 6106 became the first society engine to be moved to Didcot 11/67.
Mileage on 28/12/63, 884,490.

6697
Collett '56XX' class 0-6-2T. Built Armstrong Whitworth of Newcastle 10/1928. Cost £4,076.
Allocations: 10/28 Oxley, 4/29 Leamington, 4/60 Dowlais Cae Harris, 8/60 Barry, 9/64 Leamington, 6/65 Banbury, 11/65 Croes Newydd. Withdrawn 5/66 and sold to the Great Western Society Bristol group in working order. Kept initially at Ashchurch, it moved to Didcot 8/70.
Mileage on 28/12/63, 609,463.

6998 *Burton Agnes Hall*
Hawksworth 'Modified Hall' 4-6-0. Built Swindon 1/1949. Cost £8,529.
Allocations: 7/49 Cardiff, 3/58 Shrewsbury, 4/59 Tyseley, 4/60 Shrewsbury, 11/60 Fishguard, 1/61 Old Oak Common, 1/64 Southall, 5/65 Oxford. Withdrawn 12/65. Although officially withdrawn on 31 December 1965 the engine actually worked the last Western Region steam passenger turn between Oxford and Banbury on 3 January 1966. Purchased in running order by the Great Western Society, being kept at Totnes before moving to Didcot 12/67.
Mileage on 28/12/63, 554,089.

7202
Collett '72XX' class 2-8-2T rebuilt at Swindon 9/1934 from 2-8-0T 5277. Cost £4,580.

Allocations: 9/34 Newport Ebbw Junction, 6/42 Severn Tunnel Junction, 8/42 Newport Ebbw Junction, 4/43 Gloucester, 12/45 Severn Tunnel Junction, 3/48 Radyr, 9/62 Barry. Withdrawn 6/64 and sold to Woodham Bros, Barry. Purchased by the Great Western Society and moved to Didcot 4/74. Mileage on 28/12/63, 641,881.

7808 *Cookham Manor*
Collett 'Manor' class 4-6-0. Built Swindon 3/1938. Cost £3,986.
Allocations: 3/38 Old Oak Common, 4/39 Gloucester, 4/46 Oswestry, 12/53 Bristol (St Philips Marsh), 12/54 Gloucester, 6/59 Newton Abbot, 9/60 Exeter, 10/60 Worcester, 12/60 Tyseley, 9/62 Reading, 8/64 Swindon, 11/64 Gloucester. Withdrawn 12/65 and sold to a Great Western Society member in working order, it was kept initially at Ashchurch being moved to Didcot 8/70.
Mileage on 28/12/63, 913,744.

22
AEC streamlined Diesel Railcar. Built at Swindon 9/1940. Cost £6,240.
Allocations: 9/40 Ebbw Junction, 6/47 Worcester, 5/48 Bristol (St Philips Marsh), 12/48 Reading, 10/51 Stourbridge, 8/56 Leamington, 8/58 Worcester. Withdrawn 10/62 and sold to Great Western Society, used on Severn Valley Railway from 5/67 until being moved to Didcot 7/78. Mileages were not recorded for Diesel Railcars.

Note: Records of locomotive mileages were discontinued after 28/12/63. Cost shown is of locomotive when new. The figure, where applicable, does not include the cost of a tender.

Below:
GWR '4575' class 2-6-2T No 5572 poses on the turntable at Didcot, 29 May 1986. Built in 1929, this locomotive arrived at Didcot in 1977. *John Scrace*

Above:
2-6-2T No 6106, the first locomotive to be brought to Didcot by the Great Western Society, is shown in steam at an early open day. This locomotive was allocated to Didcot from 1935 until 1944. *D. Turner*

Below:
The only locomotive at Didcot Railway Centre to have been in the LNWR stocklist! Former Sandy & Potton 0-4-0WT *Shannon* is steamed for the first time since arrival at Didcot, 11 October 1969. *Frank Dumbleton*

Other Locomotives at Didcot

Steam Locomotives

Bonnie Prince Charlie
0-4-0ST. Built 1949. Robert Stephenson and Hawthorns. Works No 7544. Initially worked at Corralls Wharf, Poole before being moved to Corralls, Southampton where it worked until 1969. It was then purchased by The Salisbury Steam Locomotive Trust and moved to Didcot 2/69.

Pontyberem
0-6-0ST. Built by the Avonside Engine Co 1900 for the Burry Port & Gwendreath Valley Railway. Sold to Llewellyn (Nixon) Ltd (Mountain Ash Colliery) 1/1914, it was then transferred to NCB Penrikyber in 1962. Surplus to requirements it was sold to the Great Western Society 7/70 and stored at Taunton before being moved to Didcot 6/77.

5 Shannon
0-4-0WT. Built by George England & Co in 1857 for the Sandy & Potton Railway. Sold to the Wantage Tramway Co in 1878 where it worked until that line closed in 1945. The engine was then purchased by the GWR and displayed at Wantage Road station until 1964. It was then stored for a number of years, before being loaned to the Great Western Society arriving at Didcot 1/69.

Coaching Stock

- 92 Churchward auto-trailer, built 1912. Diagram U Lot 1198
- 111 Collett passenger brake van, built 1934. Diagram K41 Lot 1512
- 190 Collett auto-trailer, built 1933. Diagram A30 Lot 1480
- 212 Collett auto-trailer, built 1936. Diagram A26 Lot 1542 (originally steam railmotor 93, built 1908. Diagram R Lot 1142)
- 231 Hawksworth auto-trailer, built 1951. Diagram A38 Lot 1736
- 290 Dean four-wheel composite 1st/2nd, built 1902. Diagram U4 Lot 990
- 416 Dean four-wheel brake 3rd, built 1891. Diagram T49 Lot 582
- 484 Churchward Monster carriage truck, built 1911. Diagram P16 Lot 1191
- 536 Collett 3rd, built 1940. Diagram 77 Lot 1623
- 565 Churchward Python covered carriage truck, built 1914. Diagram P19 Lot 1238
- 814 Collett Travelling Post Office brake stowage van, built 1940. Diagram L23 Lot 1666
- 933 Dean passenger brake van, built 1898. Diagram K14 Lot 883
- 975 Dean four-wheel 3rd, built 1902. Diagram S9 Lot 992
- 1111 Collett all 3rd, built 1938. Diagram C77 Lot 1593
- 1159 Churchward passenger brake van Toplight, built 1925. Diagram K36 Lot 1344. Converted to Medical Officers' coach 1945. Diagram M33 Lot 1481
- 1184 Collett passenger brake van, built 1930. Diagram K40 Lot 1413
- 1289 Collett excursion 3rd, built 1937. Diagram C74 Lot 1575
- 1357 Dean 2nd (3rd) clerestory, built 1903. Diagram C22 Lot 1038
- 1941 Dean 3rd clerestory, built 1901. Diagram C10 Lot 962
- 2202 Hawksworth brake 3rd, built 1950. Diagram D133 Lot 1732
- 2511 Dean six-wheel family saloon, built 1894. Diagram G20 Lot 740
- 2796 Churchward Siphon G bogie milk churn van, built 1937. Diagram O33 Lot 1578
- 3299 Churchward 3rd Dreadnought, built 1905. Diagram C24 Lot 1098
- 3755 Churchward non-corridor brake 3rd City stock, built 1921. Diagram D62 Lot 1275
- 3756 Churchward non-corridor brake 3rd City stock, built 1921. Diagram D62 Lot 1275
- 4553 Collett 3rd bow ended, built 1925. Diagram C54 Lot 1352
- 5085 Collett 3rd bow ended, built 1928. Diagram C54 Lot 1383
- 5787 Collett brake 3rd, built 1933. Diagram D116 Lot 1490
- 5952 Collett all 3rd, built 1935. Diagram C67 Lot 1527
- 6824 Dean six-wheel tricomposite, built 1887. Diagram U29 Lot 370
- 7285 Collett composite, built 1941. Diagram E162 Lot 1639
- 7313 Collett composite, built 1940. Diagram E158 Lot 1621
- 7371 Collett brake composite, built 1941. Diagram E159 Lot 1640
- 7372 Hawksworth brake composite, built 1948. Diagram E164 Lot 1690
- 7976 Collett brake composite, built 1923. Diagram E114 Lot 1323
- 9002 Collett Special Saloon, built 1940. Diagram G62 Lot 1626
- 9005 Collett brake 1st saloon, built 1930. Diagram G66 Lot 1431
- 9083 Hawksworth 1st sleeping car, built 1951. Diagram J18 Lot 1702
- 9112 Collett Ocean Saloon *Queen Mary*, built 1931. Diagram G60 Lot 1471
- 9113 Collett Ocean Saloon *Prince of Wales*, built 1932. Diagram G61 Lot 1471
- 9118 Collett Ocean Saloon kitchen *Princess Elizabeth*, built 1932. Diagram H46 Lot 1471
- 9518 Dean composite diner clerestory, built 1903. Diagram H7 Lot 1010 (on chassis of 3655, built 1921)
- 9635 Collett Centenary Diner 1st, built 1935. Diagram H43 Lot 1540

Goods Wagons

1	Tar wagon, adapted for weedkilling, built Charles Roberts & Co
263	Converted to S & T mess van 1952. Diagram AA2 from 25-ton brake van 56867, built 1905 Lot 477
553	Five-plank, 10-ton, open wagon
745	Oil tank wagon — Royal Daylight, built 1912 Hurst Nelson of Motherwell
752	Special cattle van, built 1952. Diagram W17 Lot 1774 (Ashford)
2356	Fruit B fruit van, built 1892. Diagram Y1 Lot 638
2671	Bloater fish van, built 1925. Diagram S10 Lot 1356
3030	Rotank, built 1947 to carry road tank trailer. Diagram O58 Lot 1715
S4409	Six-wheel Express Dairies milk tank wagon, built Southern Railway
10153	Seven-plank, 10-ton open wagon ex-Taff Vale Railway
11152	Iron Mink 10-ton van, built 1900. Diagram V6 Lot 217
19818	Open A, built 1911. Diagram O14 Lot 632
41723	Coral A, built 1908. Diagram D2 Lot 583 (only 19 built)
41934	Crocodile F bogie well wagon, built 1909. Diagram C12 Lot 594
42193	Hydra D well wagon, built 1917. Diagram 622 Lot 745 (On loan from National Railway Museum)
42239	Grano grain van, built 1927. Diagram V20 Lot 1006
42271	Loriot L well wagon, built 1934. Diagram G13 Lot 1142
56400	Toad 14 (later 16) ton brake van, built 1899. Diagram AA3 Lot 268
63066	21-ton steel coal wagon, built 1946. Diagram N34 Lot 1480
68684	Toad 20-ton brake van, built 1924. Diagram AA15 Lot 910
79933	Tevan van, built 1921 as Mica B. Diagram X7 Lot 890. Converted to Tevan 1938. Diagram V31
80668	10-ton steel ballast wagon, built 1936. Diagram P15 Lot 1215
92943	Five-plank china clay wagon, built 1913. Diagram O13 Lot 750
94835	Open C, built between 1917 and 1927. Diagram O19. Lot 835
100377	Shunters truck, built 1923 as 10-ton van, converted 1953 Lot 882
101720	Mink A covered van, built 1924. Diagram V16 Lot 911
101836	Mink A covered van, built 1925. Diagram V14 Lot 911
105599	Banana van, built 1930. Diagram Y7 Lot 1054
105860	Mica B meat van, built 1926. Diagram X8 Lot 921
112843	Mink C express freight van, built 1931. Diagram V22 Lot 1067
116954	Asmo motor car van, built 1930. Diagram G26 Lot 1059
950592	Toad 20-ton brake van, built 1950. Diagram AA23 Lot 2099 (BR)
DW101	Drinking water tank wagon, built 1946. Diagram DD6 Lot 1555

Breakdown Train Units

1	Tool van, built 1908 Lot 570
47	Riding van, built 1908 Lot 580
56	Riding van, built 1908 Lot 571
135	Tool van, built 1908 Lot 579

Handcrane and Match Truck

205	Handcrane, built 1894 to order H2827
	Match truck, built 1930 to order H1665

Steam Cranes

23059	5-ton shunting crane, built 1954 Thomas Smith & Sons (Rodley) Ltd, Leeds
RS1054/50	50-ton breakdown crane, built 1938 Cowans Sheldon & Sons for LMS, Works No 6638

Diesel Crane

CD24	5-ton shunting crane, built 1949 Thomas Smith & Sons (Rodley) Ltd, Works No 18820

Utility Coaches

15565	BR composite, built 1955 Mk 1 Lot 30135
15577	BR composite, built 1955 Mk 1 Lot 30135

Railtour Support Coach

34671	Corridor brake 2nd, built 1955 Wolverton. Diagram AB201 Lot 30156

ADB741533 beam wagon, built Wolverton 1950 Lot 2846
Crane Runner LMS 209855
Haymarket Water Tank ADB749039, built Shildon 1950 Lot 2280

Diesel Locomotives

D1010 *Western Campaigner*
Class 52 C-C Diesel Hydraulic. Built Swindon 1962. Withdrawn 2/77 and purchased by Foster Yeoman Ltd and renamed No 1035 *Western Yeoman*. It was kept at Merehead Quarry as a static exhibit until 1986 when it was moved to Didcot. Currently being restored back into working order by the Diesel & Electric Group.

D7018
'Hymek' Class 35 B-B Diesel Hydraulic. Built by Beyer Peacock, Manchester 1962. Withdrawn 3/75, the locomotive was purchased by the Diesel & Electric Group which subsequently moved it to Didcot. After much restoration work the locomotive moved under its own power once again during 1986.

Depot Shunter DL26
0-6-0 Diesel Mechanical. Built by Hunslet, Leeds 1957. Purchased by the society from the NCB in 1978. Now used for most of the shunting work at Didcot.

Didcot Locomotive Allocations 1901

0-4-2T '517' class: 221, 549, 564, 569, 833, 846, 1425, 1467

0-6-0 'Standard Goods': 714, 715, 1190, 1208

0-6-0 'Sir Daniel' class: 471, 584

0-6-0 'Dean Goods': 2365, 2369, 2393, 2405, 2446, 2496

0-6-0ST '1016' class: 1028

0-6-0ST '1076' class: 964, 1253

0-6-0ST '1854' class: 1896

0-6-0ST '850' class: 1936, 2017

4-4-0T '3521' class: 3540, 3544

Outstabled

Wallingford
0-4-2T '517' class: 1467

Winchester
2-4-0 'River' class: 75 *Teign*
2-2-2 'Queen' class: 1117, 1130 *Gooch*
0-4-2T '517' class: 833

Total 33

Didcot Locomotive Allocations 1921

0-6-0 Armstrong 'Standard Goods': 53, 514, 779, 886, 1196

0-6-0 '360' class: 369

0-6-0T '645' class: 645

0-6-0T '1076' class: 950, 953, 1601, 1644

2-4-0 '806' class: 815, 820

0-6-0T '850' class: 995, 1912, 1927, 1953, 1996, 2002

0-6-0 'Dean Goods': 2407, 2559, 2578

2-4-0 'Stella' class: 3501, 3515

2-4-0 '3226' class: 3230

2-4-0 '3232' class: 3239, 3241, 3245, 3248

Outstabled

Lambourn
0-6-0T '850' class: 2003

Winchester
2-4-0 '3232' class: 3249
4-4-0 '3521' class: 3549

Total 32

Didcot Locomotive Allocations June 1932

0-6-0PT 'Sharp Stewart': 2190

0-6-0 'Small Goods': 908

2-4-0 'Dubs': 1334, 1335

0-4-2T '517' class: 1427, 1466

0-6-0T '850' class: 1912, 1921, 1969

0-6-0T '2021' class: 2045

0-6-0T '1076' class: 1263, 1610

0-6-0 '1813' class: 1817

0-6-0 '2251' class: 2254, 2269

0-6-0 'Dean Goods': 2303, 2395, 2397, 2405, 2430, 2450, 2463, 2512, 2532, 2549

4-4-0 'Duke' class: 3266 *Amyas*, 3267 *Cornishman*, 3269 *Dartmoor*, 3280, 3282, 3290 *Severn*, 3291 *Thames*

4-4-0 'Bulldog' class: 3356 *Sir Stafford*, 3361, 3385, 3394 *Albany*, 3448 *Kingfisher*, 3454 *Skylark*

4-6-0 'Hall' class: 4902 *Aldenham Hall*

0-6-0T 57XX class: 8768

2-6-0 'Mogul': 7306

2-6-2T '5101' class: 5101

Outstabled

Lambourn
0-6-0T '850' class: 1965

Wallingford
0-4-2T '517' class: 542

Winchester
0-6-0 'Dean Goods': 2547

Total 45

Didcot Locomotive Allocations 1960

0-6-0PT '15XX' class: 1502

0-6-0PT '57XX' class: 3622, 3653, 3709, 3721, 3751, 4649, 5744, 5746, 5783, 7772

0-6-0PT '94XX' class: 8435, 8458, 9407

0-6-0 '2251' class: 2214, 2221, 2234, 2240, 2246, 2252, 3206, 3210, 3211

2-8-0 '28XX' class: 2819, 2821, 2836, 2844

2-6-0 '43XX' class: 5337, 5351, 5380, 6379, 7324, 7327

0-6-2T '56XX' class: 5639, 5647

4-6-0 'Hall' class: 4915 *Condover Hall*, 4939 *Littleton Hall*, 4959 *Purley Hall*, 4965 *Rood Ashton Hall*, 4969 *Shrugborough Hall*, 4994 *Downton Hall*, 5943 *Elmdon Hall*, 6910 *Gossington Hall*, 6915 *Mursley Hall*, 6952 *Kimberley Hall*

4-6-0 'Modified Hall' class: 6969 *Wraysbury Hall*, 6983 *Otterington Hall*, 6996 *Blackwell Hall*

Total 48

Final Steam Allocation 14 June 1965

2-6-2T 61XX class: 6136, 6145, 6159

4-6-0 Hall class: 4962 *Ragley Hall*, 6910 *Gossington Hall*, 6921 *Borwick Hall*, 6928 *Underley Hall*, 6937 *Conyngham Hall*

4-6-0 'Modified Hall' class: 6961 *Stedham Hall*, 6963 *Throwley Hall*, 6983 *Otterington Hall*, 6991 *Acton Burnell Hall*, 7917 *North Aston Hall*

4-6-0 'Manor' class: 7814 *Fringford Manor*, 7816 *Frilsham Manor*, 7829 *Ramsbury Manor*

Total 16

On a visit to Didcot MPD by the author on Sunday 15 March 1959 the following engines were noted:

'48XX' class 0-4-2T: 1447

'57XX' class 0-6-0PT: 3622, 3652, 3653, 3709, 3751, 5737, 5744

'2251' class 0-6-0: 2218, 3210, 3212

'28XX' class 2-8-0: 2830, 2836, 2846, 3852

'City' class 4-4-0: 3440 *City of Truro*

'43XX' class 2-6-0: 5322, 5367, 5380, 5397, 6304

'56XX' class 0-6-2T: 5639, 5647, 5675, 5697

'Hall' class 4-6-0: 4939 *Littleton Hall*, 5943 *Elmdon Hall*, 6910 *Gossington Hall*, 6953 *Leighton Hall*

'Modified Hall' class 4-6-0: 6969 *Wraysbury Hall*, 6987 *Shervington Hall*, 7900 *Saint Peter's Hall*

LMS '8F' 2-8-0: 48471

'WD' 2-8-0: 90176

Total 34

Below:
One of the society's latest acquisitions is this 50-ton Cowans Sheldon steam breakdown crane, pictured here shortly after its arrival at Didcot. It was built for the LMS in 1938 (Works No 6638) and purchased by the society during 1988 from Edinburgh Haymarket.
Author

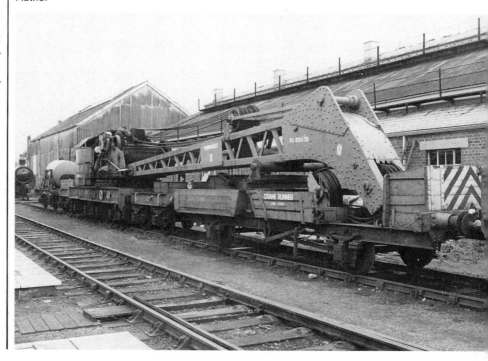